Theological Dynamics

Theological Dynamics

seward hiltner

Nashville   ABINGDON PRESS   New York

THEOLOGICAL DYNAMICS

Copyright © 1972 by Abingdon Press

ISBN 0-687-41465-2

Library of Congress Catalog Card Number: 76-186829

Scripture quotations are from the Revised Standard
Version of the Bible, copyrighted 1946 and 1952 by
the Division of Christian Education, National
Council of Churches, and are used by permission.

MANUFACTURED BY THE PARTHENON PRESS AT
NASHVILLE, TENNESSEE, UNITED STATES OF AMERICA

To
DON and LOIS DEANE
in affection and gratitude

CONTENTS

FOREWORD

For more than a dozen years Seward Hiltner has been one of the stellar faculty members of the Menninger School of Psychiatry. His unique contribution to the course of training offered to our psychiatrists and other mental health workers has been in part his erudition and his skill as a teacher and in part his sphere of expertise. No one can read the chapter headings of this book, topics of some of his most recent lectures to the Fellows in training, and fail to see their relevance and their pedagogic value for men and women seeking to become counselors of troubled people.

Who is not concerned with his first apposition—*freedom and destiny?* Who is not occasionally puzzled by the conflict of *grace and gratitude?* And as for *sin and sickness,* does a day pass when this dilemma does not present itself to attorneys, judges, jailors, or some friends of an unhappy individual? The author is interpreting theology for anyone who can read and think, but in a way that is especially important for the professions that try to help persons as persons: the clergy, physicians, psychiatrists, psychologists, nurses, social workers, guidance counselors, and others.

Why then this psychiatrist's foreword? Sometime during this lecture series Seward Hiltner asked me one day if, were he to write a book on theology for psychiatrists, I would be willing to write the foreword. I accepted promptly and, I may say, proudly. As time went on he perhaps reflected that we psychiatrists are, after all, only a handful, and while the psychologists and social workers and nurses in our field constitute somewhat larger handfuls, all of us together are not a very great company. The present book is wisely directed at a much larger audience than this group. But the author still had a collaborating psychiatrist who wanted to write a foreword for this kind of book by this kind of author.

9

Furthermore, I believe my colleagues need to read a clear, plausible, informative book in this field. Moral problems were never so challenging to psychiatry as now. Some psychiatrists may not be believers or may claim to have no interest in theological or philosophical questions. But many people *are* interested and involved in what are essentially religious, theological, moral, and philosophical matters and many do hold beliefs which influence their behavior, their thoughts, their guilt feelings, and their life purpose. These beliefs are the rightful concern of a science of the mind and of behavior and form an indispensable field of study for psychiatrists and psychologists.

Maybe the word "dynamics" in the title will attract psychiatrist readers. During my professional life that word has been a kind of shibboleth. To be really in, really "with it" in our field, one must bring "dynamic" into his conversation frequently. Just "psychology" or "psychiatry" without adjectives has reference to "the old stuff," the description of madness and insanity and mental diseases with Latin or Greek names.

But to speak of *dynamic* psychiatry or psychology is to mean something moving, something relevant to other human activities and interests. Dynamic psychiatry means a new exciting, active, effective kind of psychiatry which has something to offer people who are seeking relief or hope. Seward Hiltner uses "dynamics" in its precise Greek sense of the relationship between tensions and equilibriums. And he believes theology is dynamic in this sense. People are still seeking relief and hope and clarification from this ancient discipline as well as from some new ones. Need there be conflict?

I remember talking with Professor Ernest Southard of Harvard, one of the most brilliant psychiatrists America has ever produced, as he was leaving to give a group of addresses in New York City (at the conclusion of which he caught pneumonia and died!). As he was going down the steps of what was then called the Boston Psychopathic Hospital, he remarked to me that the trip would give him an opportunity to see a new art exhibit being shown in New York. "Psychiatry must keep abreast of all these things, you know," he said.

"Including religion?" I questioned.

"Oh yes! Yes indeed," he answered emphatically. "Religion is the most interesting field of all of them. We must discuss it together."

Unfortunately we never did. But I thought of this when a senior psychoanalytic leader and colleague from another city dropped in to my office as I was writing this foreword. We chatted about our various interests and activities and I told him about this book.

"Well, he remarked, "that is startling because one of the things I wanted to talk with you about was theology. Does that surprise you?"

"Especially the coincidence," I said. "I wasn't aware of your interest in it. Not *many* of our colleagues seem to be interested."

"I think you might be surprised how many are," said he. "They just don't talk about it."

My colleague may be right. Perhaps some who seem indifferent are rather just uncertain. They need a book like this. Even if one believes that theology deals only with myths, would we not concede that the myth is often closer to truth than is the fact? And are we or are we not in search of truth?

Seward Hiltner definitely is. And I'm with him.

KARL MENNINGER, M.D.

The Menninger Foundation
January, 1972

11

PREFACE

This book began four years ago as a series of public lectures at the Menninger Foundation on some contributions of theology to psychiatric theory. Over the previous years since 1957 when I became a consultant to the Foundation, I had often had occasion, in case conferences or other meetings, to suggest some particular contribution from theology to psychiatry and the related mental health disciplines. But until the formal lectures I had not pulled these thoughts together.

The members of my original audience were thoroughly familiar with the dynamics of human personality and of interpersonal relationships. I could therefore concentrate on the dynamics within theological doctrines, hoping that the similarity between theological dynamics and psychiatric dynamics would be sufficiently clear to interest my hearers whether or not they shared my religious views. To the first audience little was said explicitly about how my own understanding of personality dynamics has contributed to my understanding of theological dynamics, although that is a fact, and much of the idea that there is a "theological dynamics" came to me first in this way.

When I wrote up and edited this material, I realized that it was impossible for me to make any clean-cut separation of theological dynamics from personality dynamics. The content of the book is clearly focused on understanding selected theological teachings, or doctrines, dynamically. Very often the dynamic insights are drawn from theology itself. But I have no apology for the fact that, on occasion, they come from psychiatry and psychology and the related disciplines.

This is not a book about theology (or religion) and psychiatry or psychology in the sense of trying to define the areas, points of view, and functions of each, or of what they have in common, or where they differ. Theology extends to cosmic dimensions,

13

and the mental health disciplines contain many specifics. There are many writings along that theme, including some of my own. The effort of this book is different.

Both the merit and the limitation of this volume lie in its effort to delineate the ways in which theology, understood dynamically, illuminates psychology, and is in turn enriched by dynamic psychology. The religious reader should receive some help in understanding his own theology dynamically, and in some ways may broaden his knowledge of personality dynamics. The psychiatric or mental health reader may get an introduction to the dynamics of theology, and perhaps see it as making some contribution to his grasp of personality dynamics. The limitation is that dynamics represents a particular perspective upon theology and is therefore not necessarily inclusive of everything important, fundamental as I believe it to be.

As used here, dynamics comes from the Greek word for power, force, or energy. Dynamics, then, is a study of the energy components: the conflicts among energy dimensions, the tensions and counterbalances among forces, and the variety of equilibriums. Dynamics means much more than that something is not standing still. It is also, in the present discussion, more specific than a metaphysical contrast with form or shape. And in all organic life, including the human, the dynamics are far from being mechanical.

An intuitive grasp of the dynamic forces at work within persons, families, small groups, and even societies and nations, is not an invention of our own day. But the systematic study of such dynamics is comparatively recent, and it has brought rich fruit. My conviction is that theology has been intuitively wise all along (but not always right), but that with our new tools, we can see its dynamics more plainly, both to appreciate the essence of its insights, and to criticize its errors.

Although most of the doctrines, teachings, or concepts of theology are mentioned in this book, the volume would have to be several times as long in order to deal even briefly, as this book does with some doctrines, with all the major theological themes.

I am acutely aware of the fact that this book provides no

systematic treatment of the incarnation and the atonement, of creation and redemption and sanctification, of suffering, of faith, of hope, and even of God. If the present volume is well received however, it may have a sequel.

One of my helpful readers suggested that I begin the book with my chapter on general theological dynamics, instead of leaving it, as it now is, as the final chapter. For some months I was swayed by his idea and took it very seriously. But I concluded that my own way of going about things is to move from the more specific to the more general, and I should be true to my own basic way of thinking by putting the general chapter at the close. Anyone whose mind works the other way, from the more general to the more particular, may of course read Chapter Nine first.

As explained further in the text, I would not have written Chapter Five, Church and Community, at all, without the helpful prodding of James Luther Adams. He forced me to move into an area beyond my realm of special competence. But he was right. That chapter was essential to this book. It may demonstrate some of my vulnerabilities, but it also shows my concern that extends beyond any conceivable kind of pietism.

One of my readers rendered his opinion that my book was "confessional" in nature. My initial reaction to this comment was argumentative. Was I not attempting to state the faith (in some dimensions at least) so that believers could better understand it, and others might take another look at it? If "confessional" should be understood as simply adopting a position and then trying to "sell" it to those who do not agree, I would certainly wince. But if "confessional" means coming clean both about what I believe and what I doubt, then the label makes good sense to me. It may well be, as the thoughtful reader implied, that I have told here more of my personal faith than I realized I was doing. So long as this kind of confessional dimension does not get in the way of my dynamic analyses, I am quite ready to accept the confessional label.

Except for the original lectures at the Menninger Foundation, few parts of this book have been used in oral presentation except for four lectures at the University of Utrecht in Holland during the autumn of 1970, and at the pastors' seminar of the United Methodist Church of Kansas in early 1971. I want to express appreciation to the key persons in all these institutions for giving me valuable feedback that has helped me to complete the editing of this book.

I am deeply thankful to my friend of thirty years, Karl Menninger, for writing the Foreword to the book, and for his valuable comments on the manuscript at various stages. This Preface itself has profited greatly from his injunction to get right down to it and to say what I mean.

My thanks are also large to other colleagues at the Menninger Foundation who read my material and offered useful suggestions about it, including Kenneth R. Mitchell, Paul W. Pruyser, and Philip Woollcott. Others whose comments have been influential in the final editing of the book include my Princeton Seminary colleague, James N. Lapsley; and Francis J. Braceland, editor of the *American Journal of Psychiatry*; James Luther Adams, just retired from the Harvard Divinity School; Mallary Fitzpatrick, of the Hartford Seminary Foundation; and James A. Knight, of Tulane University.

I am much indebted to Lillabelle Stahl, assistant secretary of the Menninger Foundation, for technical help with the manuscript and for soliciting critical comments on it from various people. Elaine Apple, my former secretary at Princeton Seminary, helped by duplicating the material.

SEWARD HILTNER

Princeton Theological Seminary
    and The Menninger Foundation

October, 1971

Chapter 1
FREEDOM AND DESTINY

It may appear odd to the reader that the title of the first chapter is not headed "God" and, since the writer is a Christian, that the ensuing chapter is not about "Jesus Christ." I promise that God and Jesus Christ and some things one might expect will appear in due course in the content of the book. But the fact is that the doctrines or teachings of theology may be organized in various ways. And since my principal purpose is to demonstrate the dynamics of theology with special help from psychology and related disciplines, I have chosen a plan of organization calculated to that end.

In the last chapter of the book I have discussed my general conception of theology and theological method, and of the potential contribution of dynamic psychology to theological understanding. All the other chapters are focused on some specific theological teaching. In each chapter heading I have linked the doctrine with a particular kind of human problem or potentiality. Regardless of the reader's views about religion and theology, I assume him to be concerned about freedom, gratitude, trust, sickness, community, sexuality, and death. In each instance I shall attempt to show the close connection between these areas of human concern and specific theological doctrines.

In the present chapter the discussion will begin with freedom, and move on later to destiny. There seem to be three principal ways in which theology has approached the freedom question, and these will be dealt with in turn. Although they are interrelated and not divorced from one another, much is lost if they are simply collapsed together. Each of them speaks to a different level of freedom. In the order in which they appeared historically, these three dimensions of, or insights into,

human freedom are, in my own words: freedom as self-fulfillment, freedom as self-direction, and freedom as self-transcendence.

Freedom as Self-Fulfillment

It is freedom as self-fulfillment which the New Testament
discusses, commends, and rejoices in. The letters of Paul are
full of statements, rejoicings, even ejaculations, about the new
condition that has come to the people who are in Jesus Christ.[1]
Always in the background, and sometimes articulated, is some
form of previous bondage which the new freedom in Christ
has conquered. The pole concept to freedom in the sense of
fulfillment is, therefore, previous bondage or enchainment.
Now that one has something that is radically better, he is exultantly aware of how he was previously enchained. The dimension of feeling is, therefore, very prominent in this aspect of
freedom.

Most often Paul, as a Jew, rejoiced that he had, through
Christ, been liberated from bondage to the law.[2] Paul knew
quite well that the high Jewish law was itself liberating and
not enslaving. It simply represented the guidelines that man
should follow in keeping his part of the covenant that God
had made with Israel, and in return for which God gave not
only justice but also mercy. But Paul had seen the law turned
into enormously detailed laws, so that the Jew trying to live a
good life seemed always to be doing this or that commanded
in detail, or avoiding something else that was prohibited. Since
this kind of legalism made man initially wary and then later
proud, Paul saw that it was a kind of chain. The big thing was
forgotten in the details.

From modern dynamic psychologies like that of Freud we
have learned much about the kind of bondage represented in
the law in Paul's understanding. In extreme form we would
now call this obsessionalism or perfectionism, the person striv-
ing valiantly to meet some internal and rigid standard, never
really succeeding, and thus devoid of any joy in life.[3] In less
extreme forms we speak of compulsive behavior, such as un-

comfortableness unless everything is neat, or uneasiness if one departs from a fixed schedule. We believe the dynamics to be similar in the extreme and the moderate instances. Somewhere in earlier life the person has been rewarded negatively for his natural mild experiments with disorder or spontaneity or disobedience. He then tries to cope with these partial rejections by conforming to the nth degree. For his conformist behavior he may or may not receive praise, but he does avoid disapprobation. Thus his life patterns come to focus around doing whatever will avoid disapproval. Since the pattern is set in early life, much of its content will become irrelevant by the time he reaches mature years. But in one degree or another he will continue his strategy of appeasement. The focus of his perception will be on negativity and avoidance. Hence, his perceptions are unlikely to be open to joyfulness or other positive feelings.

Paul saw that it was much more important to be a liberated man than a good man.[4] For the obsessional effort always to be good (not to merit disapproval), or the smug illusion that one has achieved goodness (no disapprobation forthcoming), are both marks of bondage. Of course Paul's relegation of human goodness to a secondary position did not mean that he advocated acting on whim or discarding the hard-won moral principles of the Jewish people. To use Freudian language, Paul's intuition at this point was about the severe damage done when a person's whole life remains under the dominance of his Superego. Whether he is jittery or smug, we would regard such a person or group today as warping the totality of psychic life in order to appease one dimension.

Paul wrote less often about it, but on the other side he also believed that a libertine life was a form of bondage.[5] Especially to the little Christian group in Corinth he wrote scathingly about their way of interpreting their freedom in Christ. Because they believed themselves to be free in Jesus Christ, they assumed that anything goes, probably including promiscuous sexual relationship and even homosexual behavior. Paul had to write in strong terms to show them that such a misconception was itself a form of bondage.

19

Dynamic psychologies have, of late years, also taught us something of what happens when libertarianism takes over. In the early days of psychoanalysis, Freud's patients were mostly under bondage to the law of an outmoded Superego.[6] In recent years, however, a large proportion of mental patients, especially among younger people, has been free to the point of libertarianism about matters like sexual behavior. But this kind of false freedom has not prevented them from becoming enemies to their society and to themselves.[7] Sometimes the dynamics of these conditions arise from defective conscience formation. Perhaps more often, they contain partially hidden compulsions, as in the promiscuous girl who is getting back at either or both of her parents. Some of the extreme libertarian behavior of a segment of modern teen-agers shifts the object of contempt from the parents and their standards to the culture as a whole, and justifies its compulsive libertarianism in the name of some kind of new community.

In the instance of the latter group especially, but also of the individuals who have got into enough trouble to warrant hospital treatment, we need to caution ourselves against mere condemnation. As Charles Reich suggests, there may be in some groups of young people the dawn of a new "consciousness" or conception of human values that is, however unadmittedly, related to Christian conceptions.[8] But the more libertarian the conduct, the greater the chance that compulsion rather than a new consciousness is at work.

When Paul's insights about human bondage (to the law or to the anti-law) are reflected on in the light of modern knowledge of dynamics, a general insight appears about the time-perspective in relation to bondage, no matter what its specific nature. Some forms of bondage, like a toothache or unhappiness in marriage or overt anxiety, show their true character as bondage while one is still chained to them. But others do not, like the cancer without pain, or the anxiety that has gone underground into a minor but rarely painful symptom, or the joyless defiance that comes from disillusionment.

Bondage that is felt as such is insistent upon some kind of remedial action. The action taken may be wise, or it may try to eliminate the symptoms without dealing with the underlying condition. Just as in Paul's day, however, the principal bondages are those not felt as such, or felt so only ambiguously, so that a clear call to change and action is not heard from the conditions themselves. For us as for Paul, it would be false to assert that everything is just fine if we are feeling no pain. And yet with many people and groups, in our day as well as Paul's, bondage may be perceived clearly only if the person or the group have already begun to emerge from it.

In pastoral counseling it is a common experience at the beginning that the person or couple view their problem as very limited, but that, after a few sessions of competent counseling, he or they come to realize that the problem has been more pervasive than could previously be admitted. Such a recognition is in itself a mark that progress has been made. Only in a more secure retrospect could the reality of past enchainments be seen with clarity.

When people are in them, neither legalism nor libertarianism signal themselves clearly as bondage. Thus, in his dealing with both kinds of groups, Paul apparently realized that only in their new condition could they become deeply aware of the nature of their previous bondage. When they did not reach this point spontaneously, he went after them hammer and tongs to get the point. Whether the factor that produces experiential change is commitment to Jesus Christ, psychiatric therapy, or something else, the most severe bondages in human life are likely to be seen in their true character only when there has been at least the beginning of release from them. Retrospective appraisal, especially after positive change, is much more to be trusted than is evaluation during the situation.

If one tries too hard to forget, and sets wholly out of his mind the nature and intensity of the previous bondage, an error is being made. The alcoholic addict who forgets what just one drink can do is back on the treadmill. The person who has had a difficult problem in dealing with authority figures and who has improved his relationships is in much better shape if he can occasionally recall the trouble he got into previously.

If he does not do so, he may alternate between obsequiousness and arrogance, and get into new troubles.

There is, then, even in the freedom of self-fulfillment, some aspect of reflective checkup. One ought not to be obsessed by the old problem, but neither should he be under compulsion to forget it altogether. The Alcoholics Anonymous program has picked up this insight very well especially in its Twelfth Step, according to which nondrinking members devote serious time to helping other alcoholics.[9] This procedure provides a kind of built-in reminder about the bondage from which, so far, the person has been released. If the recovered alcoholic, or indeed anyone else who has got rid of his particular chains, should come to regard his new condition as simply natural and normal, with no reflection on the way in which he had once been in bondage, he would be quite likely to fall again, perhaps without knowing it at the time since its form might be different.

Both in pastoral counseling and in psychiatric or psychological therapy, some conclusions follow from the insight indicated. Termination procedures usually include reference to trusting and also testing the gains, and watching the signals that may suggest a return for more help.[10] Even in the ordinary instance, however, I believe that these practices could be added to helpfully by some explicit discussion about reflecting on present problems and freedoms in the light of past bondages. Warning may well be given that an obsessive preoccupation with past bondages, or a compulsive attempt to forget them altogether, are both equally signs that the new condition is precarious, and more help may be needed.

The aspect of freedom that has been called here self-fulfillment, and which we have been illustrating mainly from Paul but also from psychological and psychiatric experience, has some counterpart in most religious groups, and tends to be most prominent when the groups are young or eager or both, and when the kind of bondage from which they have been released is salient and evident and has not faded into dim clouds of early history. Such groups differ vastly in the degree to which they simply feel their release experience without much reflection, as against their attempt to preserve the advance by serious occasional analysis of what happened before. Where a group is concerned, it plainly makes a lot of difference if the group simply interprets its release as an excuse to avoid contact with the world, or if it interprets its new freedom as calling for involvement with the world in a new way.

The freedom of self-fulfillment begins as a sigh of thanks or rejoicing, as a kind of prayerful expulsion of breath. How awful, we now see, was the situation back there! Yet the rejoicing and the sighing are not enough. There must also be reflection, from time to time, on the nature and meaning of the new freedom, and also on the bondage from which one has now been released. If there were no such reflection, then the whole thing would soon fade into obscurantism under the guise of, "This is the way things are." The neglect of history is fatal.

Important as it is with its experience-centered focus on the new feeling and the old bondage, the freedom of self-fulfillment has limits. It is not the whole of freedom. The person or group who has gone thus far must go farther to additional reflection. In the course of time, the new condition tends to fade into the "way things are." At this stage there may be a lesser capacity to differentiate between the old and the new.

Terms like "surrender" have sometimes been used in theology in order to prevent the fadings after the honeymoon of the new freedom has lost its novelty. Such terms ought not to be misinterpreted as if they simply meant bowing legalistically before the demands of the Superego.

In a religious group, then, especially one that is new and authentic, freedom felt as release from this or that kind of bondage tends to come first. The extent to which serious reflection by the group will follow from the experience depends upon many factors: constitution of the group, its ideas, its leadership, and the way in which others question it. But if there is no deep and searching reflection, the group may fall into some form of bondage as bad as that from which the religious experience released it. The tests of its freedom of self-fulfillment are likely to come afterward, in whether it does or does not apply systematic procedures of reflection.

On the other side, however, it is essential to freedom in the self-fulfillment sense that there be a mood and feeling of release and joy. A group whose reflections lead only to dirges and not also to rejoicings would be suspect. Even though positive feeling is not in the long run a sufficient element in testing the freedom of self-fulfillment, it is necessary as a mood.

We may draw a final conclusion from the discussion of freedom in the dimension of self-fulfillment. Since theology is not a mere combination of ritualism and moralism, it is concerned with the potential release of men from *any* kind of bondage they are in, whether while in it they recognize or not that it *is* bondage. Not that theology or the church are necessarily the technologists who can produce that release, for most often they are not. But the church concerns itself with all forms of bondage and release from them, no matter what technologies are necessary to bring release. Human bondage is enchainment whatever its specifics, and God himself welcomes all human effort to release men.

Freedom as Self-Direction

It was very early in the history of Christian theology that the elementary reflections on freedom as release from bondage moved on to the question of freedom as self-direction. To what degree, if at all, does a man determine himself, and to what extent is he simply molded and formed by forces over which he has no control? What kind of control if any does mankind have over itself?

As soon as there were philosophers. they fought over this kind of freedom question. Later, when there were scientists and psychologists, they fought over it also. The first point about consideration of the question by theology, however, is that it was anteceded by felt and partially reflected-on experiences of freedom as release from palpable bondage. That sequence has not always been true of the work of either philosophers or scientists.

When the question about freedom is self-direction or its denial, then the context is not bondage, as in the freedom of

24

self-fulfillment, but causality or its modern equivalents. If the person and group really have the power to decide and determine this and that about themselves, then the answer is in terms of a positive power of self-direction. If, on the other hand, such apparent self-determination can be demonstrated as illusory, then it follows that both man and mankind have little capacity in fact for self-direction.[11]

It is important to understand the context in which the question of freedom as self-direction arose in Christian thought. Up to a point, the course followed was borrowed from the Jews.[12] In their understanding of creation, the Jews believed that man was made as an animal in every sense of the word including the gastronomical, the sexual, and the thanatological. Thus man was clearly a creature and not a self-creation. To be sure, man was held to have some kind of dominion over other creatures of the world.[13] But because he was believed to have been made in the image of God, man was declared to have not so much power as the capacity for love and for freedom.[14] That is, man was believed, on the one hand, to be animal like other creatures of God, but also, on the other hand, to have the capacity for relationship with God through worship and prayer and service of fellowman. And at the same time, man was believed to have a degree of freedom far exceeding that of other creatures, even though it is limited and not of the order of God's own freedom. These points about freedom as self-direction came from Judaism.

The ancient Jews also noticed a worm in the existential apple. To what extent were Adam and Eve really free to decide between what God had enjoined upon them as against what the serpent enticed? When in fact they chose the latter, the implication was, at the very least, that the exercise of freedom was ambiguous. To be sure, the Jewish creation accounts are profound, and these remarks do not do them full justice.[15] But for our present purpose the point of them is that the accent fell upon the ambiguities of decision rather than upon whether or not it was possible. Indeed, the accounts in Genesis simply assume the reality of freedom as self-direction. Their focus lies elsewhere, in the undesirable consequences.

THEOLOGICAL DYNAMICS

By the time that Christians in the second century A.D. and later came to consider the doctrine of creation, they fortunately accepted all the essentials from their Jewish ancestors. Like the writers of Genesis, they were mainly appalled at how bad affairs can become when man exercises his freedom of choice. They nevertheless saw man's freedom, along with his capacity for relationship, as special gifts of God even when they were misused. But unlike the early Jewish writers, they lived in an intellectual environment in which the question about the degree of man's capacity for self-direction was asked in a serious and general sense. And so, from then on, they became concerned with both questions, not only that of the consequences of man's choices but whether in fact his apparent decisions were what they seemed to be.

The great early theological writer about freedom was Augustine in the fourth century.[16] His main point was much like the Old Testament. He held that man has freedom of self-direction in a sense but that what he chooses is always wrong. His hope, according to Augustine, lies in his commitment of himself and his choices to God through Jesus Christ. If he does so, it is no longer the old person who is making the decisions.

From then on Augustine had to wrestle with the question of whether, once a man has committed himself to God in Christ, the decisions are really his or not. If he said that they are then made by God, of course man would appear like a robot, and the reality of sin would have been impugned in terms of man's responsibility. So he had to say that the choices of the new man in Jesus Christ are his own. But Augustine's awareness of the continuing presence of sin leading to wrong choices was so lively that the point of emphasis was always that our choices are relatively free but wrong. But in however subsidiary a way, it had to be conceded that man has some capacity for self-direction, in however misguided a way he may exercise it.[17]

As we shall see in more detail in the chapter on sin, persons like Augustine were not trying to condemn man for deciding wrongly. They recognized what has been called an "original"

26

or collective dimension about sin which is not unlike our modern recognition that an underprivileged child of the slums is worked against by many given forces not of his own making. The focal concern of an Augustine was, however, about where a person may turn to get guidance in exercising the potential power of choice in self-direction, no matter what others have done to him. In other words, the focus was on therapy and change beginning now. Where, now, do we turn for guidance on our self-direction? More sophisticated, this view is nevertheless basically the same as that found in Genesis.

The subsequent great leaders of Christian thought before the modern period—Anselm, Thomas, Calvin, and Luther especially—mostly followed the position that the important fact was man's misusing his freedom of self-direction.[18] Their discussions have at times been misinterpreted as if they denied that man could, freely, pass the salt across the table. On all such trivial or secondary questions, they simply assumed man's capacity for self-direction. One is likely to live even if he does not get the salt. But the question whether a man or group can determine those basic and ultimate matters upon which their destiny depends, that was the level at which the question was approached. And the fundamental answer they all gave was no. Man has some real power of self-direction, but he is altogether likely to misuse it in fundamental matters unless he has a guide: in grace, in Jesus Christ, or in the church.

In some contrast to the discussions of freedom as self-direction in older philosophical circles and more recent scientific groups, it must be admitted that the preoccupation of most of our theological forebears was on the point of what people do with their freedom of self-direction, not whether or not they have any. As a matter of fact, insofar as theological groups have set forth positions on the more general question of how much freedom of self-direction a man or a group actually has, the answers have varied greatly. It is true that no theological position has ever denied some capacity for self-direction, for that would attribute all evil and sin to God. But no position has ever held man to be complete master of his fate and destiny, for that would deny God's function in human life and would probably also deny the sense in which human communities are interdependent under God.

In the later discussion of providence and predestination, we shall return to the issue of man's capacity for self-direction. But we may note here that even in Calvinism, which above all other theologies saw man's life as directed or guided by God, the intent was mainly to show that the other-directing forces are not blind or ambiguous but benevolent.[19] Calvinists believed, on the one side, that you were really free to pass or not pass the salt, and they believed, on the other side, that the universal forces determining our destiny are more friendly than alien. In between, they assumed we could direct a lot about ourselves, and their concern was with how we did it.

Today it seems evident that answers to the question about the extent to which a man directs himself must draw upon detailed data not available to our forebears, theological or otherwise. We have a few complete other-determinists today, who render themselves suspect by the vehemence of their arguments and their tendency to regard responsibility as merely epiphenomenal, that is, as emerging automatically once some needs are met.[20] We have also a few self-determinists who generally neglect the infantile psychic residues in all adult human beings, the ambiguities of aggressive impulses, and even the realities of conditioning. Most thoughtful people today, including scientists, do not profess to take extreme positions on the question. For example, the psychiatrist who knows that there are no mere accidents in human psychic life nevertheless also realizes that, for himself or his patients, there are realms where genuine choice is possible.[21] What modern knowledge is beginning to illuminate is the specific conditions needed for constructive choice and change. Thus, the contribution of modern knowledge to answering the question about the degree of our self-determination is basically to substitute a new question, namely, what are the situation and conditions?

Dynamic factors are much involved in answers given to the question of freedom as self-direction. If one believes that his life is wholly determined by forces other than himself, then his feeling about life is likely to rest upon whether or not he believes those other forces to be benevolent. Should he believe them to be malignant or ambiguous, he can summon at best a kind of existentialist defiance or courage to combat them. If he believes them benevolent but omnipotent, then he is quite likely to deny or deprecate the areas of freedom that lie before him, and in one sense be irresponsible about them.

If he believes, on the other hand, that he can determine everything important about his life, sooner or later he is in for a rude awakening. No matter how protected he is by learning, profession, wealth, or ability, it is certain that some day other-directed events will affect his cocoon.

Most people are at neither extreme. And yet they have not generally reflected on: (1) how they should respond in the event of tragic change such as fatal illness in a spouse or child; (2) an upward event, such as a promotion, that carries with it new responsibilities as well as new privileges. Of course such startling experiences can, in a sense, be met only on their occurrence. But their ubiquity in human life suggests that it would not be out of place to consider them generally in advance. When this is done, the extravagance of either the fate theory or the fully self-determining theory becomes patently inadequate. What seems best calculated to help with coping in all such situations, up or down, is a combination of flexible principles, courage, and pragmatic ability to analyze the actual situation and the potentialities that could appear in light of this or that course of action.

As indicated earlier, there have been different positions in Christian history about the degree to which a man directs himself though always with an avoidance of the extreme positions. The main point of all such discussions in theology, however, has not been with yes or no as to self-direction, but with the consequences assuming at least some degree of self-direction.

Perhaps, in the data fed to a modern computer, there may be potential material for determining the extent to which this or that decision was self- or other-determined. Let us suppose that the personal decision element was only four percent, while the other-determined aspects were ninety-six percent.

29

This situation might be like the two gallons of water invaded by the one ounce of red dye. A decisive difference might very well rest upon four percent. Certainly this would be true if the question were about color.

What theology has been concerned about is, I believe, a way of distinguishing between self- or other-direction at points where genuine and positive changes have occurred, and those where this has not happened. The person who has absorbed and assimilated some compulsion from his past, for instance, through counseling or psychotherapy, is not the same person who was subjected to those external influences to begin with. The process of assimilating one's personal history with all its good and bad elements, and also of revaluing one's values in the present, alters the degree of self-direction that the person has. About all that we know about this process is that the person who comes to terms with his past in psychic honesty, and reads the future in the light of this historical assimilation, has a better chance of both planning for and adapting to the future.

We might put it in this way: the freedom of self-direction is real only as it is developed, and risked. Perhaps this appears to be a more contingent answer to the question than was given by many of our ancestors. Yet they too seldom took extreme positions. They did believe, as we do today, that man's freedom is limited but very real. What modern knowledge adds is some grasp of the conditions under which more self-direction may appear.

I have tried to show that theology has never become completely stuck on the question of whether man determines himself or not. He is not a robot but he has limits. The crucial question has been held to be: what does man do with the capacity for decision that he has? The answer has generally been: not much that is constructive. Hence, there has always been a call to repentance or, in modern terms, an invitation to change perspective in examining every decision.

Theology has no final theoretical opinion about how much self-direction exists in persons or groups. Any man's freedom is both safeguarded and limited by the groups and instituttions of which he is a part. So his capacity for self-direction always has many limits upon it, and yet it is very real. In a complex situation, one may have only a small percentage of control over the many factors. But if this tiny amount is like the bit of red dye in a large vat of water, it may nevertheless determine the color of the whole. It requires empirical investigation to show how much capacity for self-direction exists in this person or that group. But I believe the theological approach to the question provides an intelligible framework for such studies. For one must move on from asking about the degree of control to the even more important question of how the freedom is used.

Freedom as Self-Transcendence

When freedom is understood as release from bondage, it is felt more or less unambiguously as a good thing. When it is understood as the negation of complete determination by outside forces, then too it is usually viewed as a good in itself no matter how many mistakes its exercise may produce. Yet we cannot say that either of these first two aspects of freedom, when reflected on, is devoid of ambiguity. If release from bondage is to be genuine, there must be reflection from time to time on the bondage, and checking up on the release. If some freedom of self-direction is present, then it is precisely the misuse of this freedom that may produce the real difficulties.

It remained for relatively more recent theologians, notably Kierkegaard, to package all the ambiguous aspects of human freedom into the notion of self-transcendence.[22] There are problems with this term, for it is really a horizontal metaphor, whereas in common speech it is used as if the reference were vertical. The real meaning, "moving across," must be kept in mind if the theological intent is to be understood.

In freedom understood as self-transcendence, the rejoicing that we found in the freedom of self-fulfillment becomes qualified. Even though our faith has granted us some new vision, this does not protect us from the anxiety and even terror of making decisions, since we can foresee only part of their consequences. Therefore, decisions need to be confronted soberly rather than exultantly. There may be a time for rejoicing, but it comes later, not at the ambiguous point of decision.

As to the freedom of self-direction, Kierkegaard agreed with the tradition that, despite our limitations, we have a lot of it. He also agreed that our guidelines for decision should be taken from God's revelation to mankind. His originality lay in noting the ambivalent feeling dimensions of any man or group that takes this task seriously.

Kierkegaard used the metaphor of the abyss or chasm. As a man realizes that he has just made a decision, he looks into the future of all the decisions yet to be made, and that situation appears to him like an abyss. So he is gravely tempted to retreat from the brink, to find shelter in the mores of his group, in an intellectual system, or in anything that will protect him from the burden of using his freedom in decisions. So Kierkegaard understood the basic temptation. What *ought* we to do under these circumstances? What we should do is to exercise our freedom in full awareness of its fallibility. Only so can we move toward becoming genuinely human, trying to learn from our decision mistakes as well as thanking God when our decision has proved retrospectively good.

Our fundamental freedom of self-transcendence is, then, not so much something to be won as something to be acknowledged in its ambiguity, and then courageously pursued. As Kierkegaard himself did, we may look to God and God's revelation for guidelines as we use our freedom. But there is nothing in those guidelines that automatically alleviates our anxiety, assures us in advance that we are right, or makes our decisions easy.

Let us examine what this kind of position means when we are dealing with specific situations. Suppose that a man has had the benefit of advanced education of the best kind. Any time he confronts a contemporary matter, he is able to see it in the light of the cultural past, and he will have at least some capacity to predict how it may turn out in the future. Thus, he is more free, and less bound, by the event itself than is the person of limited education. To use the jargon, he has more capacity to transcend the event and even his own involvement in it. Thus, his freedom of self-direction is greater. But how does he use this freedom?

Or consider another man deeply troubled by a crippling emotional illness of some kind, who has found the courage to do what is necessary therapeutically about it. While under the chains of the illness, he was almost wholly preoccupied with it. Now that time and genuine effort have intervened, he is free to look at things—trees and books and people and much more—as he could not do before. He transcends himself now to a degree that he could not do while under the burden of illness. But what, now, does he do with the new freedom?

Let us face it. The well-educated man and the man whose therapy has been successful may both use their freedom to avoid social responsibility, to make themselves as secure as life permits, and even at times to gain power over other people. Or such a person may become a kind of dilettante not focusing on anything in particular, or be sympathetic to people who went through what he did and contemptuous of all others.

As Kierkegaard saw, the gain in freedom brings on new ambiguities. The latter fact is no reason at all to impede the increase of freedom. Freedom is basically a good. Indeed, its development is indispensable to truly human functioning. But if its problems as well as its gains are not rightly appraised, it turns on itself and makes life harder for both persons and society.

Nearly twenty years ago at the University of Chicago Bernard M. Loomer and I offered a joint seminar on the relation of theology to the psychiatric and psychological disciplines. One of the reading assignments was Dorothy Baruch's *One Little Boy*, a detailed account of therapy with a very much disturbed child from the ages of seven to thirteen.[23] The therapy was well done and the book was well written, and the improvement remarkable in the little boy's condition. At the close, he was even able to accept his parents along with their particular neuroses. Our seminar tried to analyze the factors that had been influential in increasing the boy's freedom.

At that point Loomer startled us all by asking, "But isn't

there something monstrous about a child who can look con-
descendingly at his parents?" Loomer intended no criticism
of the therapy and no denigration of the boy's increase in freedom. He simply meant that a child who could look conde-
scendingly on his parents could conceivably look in detachment at other people and other predicaments, and thus use
his freedom primarily for purposes of self-protection and non-
involvement. Thus, even though an increase in freedom is
always to be desired, its actualization may lead to patterns and
decisions that are far from desirable.

To show the meaning, the desirability, and yet the ambiguity
of man's freedom understood as self-transcendence, I have used
illustrations that show gains in this capacity through recognizable means like education and therapy. What can we say about
this quality in people with no therapy, little education, and
perhaps not very much intelligence? On the question of the
degree to which basic capacity is or is not present, it is plain
that theologians must defer to psychologists and other investi-
gators. But theology would hold that some degree of this
capacity is present in all human beings.[24] The demonstration
in recent years that this capacity can be increased by good
education, even in persons of low intelligence, helps to support
the theological view. It is man's self-transcendence that pre-
vents him, so to speak, from becoming merely an animal no
matter how hard he may try. His standard trans-animal equipment may not have had much development, but it is still
present.

In seeking the remote origins of the insight into freedom as
necessary but ambiguous, tribute must certainly be paid to
classical Greek thought and its understanding of reason as the
unique attribute of mankind. Later, the theological position
saw that reason, while important, is an insufficient way of
getting at the capacity that constitutes the uniqueness of the
human race. Man's self-transcendence depends upon no one
characteristic of psychic life, but upon knowledge, mental
health, ego-strength, and many other qualities that normally
go along with positive human development.[25]

When we examined freedom as self-fulfillment, we saw that its context was bondage or restriction. With freedom as self-direction, the context was causality or the modern sophisticated equivalents. With freedom seen as self-transcendence, it is more difficult to pinpoint the context precisely because of the emphasis on ambiguities. Probably the best statement that can be made is that, the freer the man, the greater and more accurate his perceptiveness. As we have already noted, however, perceiving must be accompanied by courage if the free man is to use his ability in becoming truly human.

Self-transcendence is a more comprehensive way of understanding man's freedom than is self-fulfillment or self-direction. It has the additional merit of using the data of the theological discussion of self-direction, finally asking what we are doing with the freedom we do have. The great danger of understanding freedom as self-transcendence is in the possibility of losing the very joy that the New Testament regarded as fundamental to freedom. Life and decisions may seem such burdens that detachment finally becomes the rule, and then the potentialities for joy and self-fulfillment are swallowed up in anxiety and prudence. Hence, even though our main concept of freedom should involve the fact of self-transcendence, it is at the peril of not becoming human that we lose freedom understood as joyful release from bondages of various kinds.

The dynamic advantage that freedom as self-transcendence has over the other dimensions is that in it the dynamics are acknowledged in the conception. One is simultaneously allured to use his freedom and to retreat from it, and even when he advances into use of the freedom, he may retreat in the character of his decisions to the detriment of himself or others. One of the reasons why this conception needs always to be balanced by freedom understood as self-fulfillment is that here the emphasis is put on the positive side of using freedom responsibly although not infallibly. Rightly understood, freedom should be responsible and clear-eyed about ambiguities, but it should also bring joy and gratitude rather than anxious detachment.

THEOLOGICAL DYNAMICS

Destiny as Polar to Freedom

It is Paul Tillich to whom I am indebted for the concept of destiny as polar to freedom in the most comprehensive sense, as against the other poles that are useful in relation to various dimensions of freedom: bondage in relation to self-fulfillment, causality or other-determination in relation to self-direction, and perceptiveness plus courage in relation to self-transcendence.[26]

At any point in the life of a man or a people, destiny depends upon two kinds of factors: first, the limits imposed by the consequences of previous experiences and decisions; second, the capacities to be self-transcendent and self-directive that still inhere. Thus Tillich saw destiny as a combination of both kinds of factors, limiting and releasing.

Such a view avoids the idea of fate on the one side and of absence of consequences on the other. Fate implies that nothing can be changed. It is shown, for example, in the Oedipus story where Oedipus killed a man along the road, not knowing that the man was his father. From then on the whole future course of events was fated, sealed, and inevitable. The destiny idea holds that, even though the past puts limits on the present and hence on the future, both present and future have genuine aspects of freedom especially if the person or group understands and deals forthrightly with the limitations.

The other advantage of the destiny idea is its escape from the folly of not envisaging consequences. If I decide to become a preacher or a plumber, for whatever reasons good or bad, I cannot also then become a physician or a banker. And my decision is meaningful only to the extent that I grasp such a notion at the time the decision is made.

The possible disadvantage of the term "destiny" is that it may connote only something final, away off there in time. But I believe we can domesticate it, as Tillich did, to show that, at any point of decision about the future, there is a certain combination of factors involving both limitation and freedom, and that the wisest way to get ahead is to acknowledge both kinds forthrightly.

Destiny provides a way of looking, at any point, in our individual or collective lives, at what is still open to us and what is, for all practical purposes, closed because of previous events and decisions. What we are now is determined not only by the other-determining factors such as our parents and our culture and our church and our education, but also by the consequences of the choices we have made in the light of both these background factors and whatever our freedom of self-direction has been able to add—including our particular response to the terror and ambiguity of having to make decisions at all. But there are still openness and freedom. Our capacity to see where they lie is greatly dependent upon our ability to see and understand what is closed to us because of our history. The more accurately we can analyze both the closed and the open sides, the more freedom will be evident in our decisions.

Chapter 2
GRACE AND GRATITUDE

In a general sense, the theological concept of grace is a kind of saintly and ultimately important serendipity. It registers belief in and experience of improbably fortunate events. It is not just a vote for good luck. It has stability because God is its author. And it is not about trivialities or ephemeralities, which we can handle ourselves without special assistance. Theology holds that, were not grace at work, beyond all our planning or other effort, our human plight would be impossible.

Important as it is, however, grace in its basic meaning is little understood and little experienced even among faithful Christians. The principal reason for this fact, I have come to believe, is that so little attention has been devoted to the human response to grace, and thus, even when God's grace is clearly at work, there are few tools and concepts to guide our response and hence even our understanding of the reality. By an analysis of genuine gratitude, this discussion will attempt to make up for that usual omission.

An Introduction on Terms

The Latin word for grace is *gratia*.[1] In the plural, *gratiae*, it means thanks. Obviously gratitude comes from the same root. I shall try to show the profundity of this connection and to demonstrate that it is impossible to understand the human response to grace without grasping the meaning of genuine gratitude and separating it from its distortions.

The Greek word for grace is *charis*, which means both grace and thanks, and which survives in English today in words like charismatic. *Charis* is very close to joy. In the Old Testament the Hebrew forerunner of *charis* is *hesed*, which is usually translated to mean pity. But in later Judiasm *hesed* means something closer to *charis*.

Since the meanings behind both grace and gratitude center about thankfulness, it is interesting to find that in most of the Indo-European languages there is both a conventional and a serious word for thanks. The former would be applied if some one were asked to pass the salt and did so. The latter would be employed only when something important had been done. The most amusing conventional word for thanks is in the Lithuanian *ačiū*, which is pronounced like a sneeze and which came to mean, "Good luck, God bless you!"

Grace as Evoking Thanks

The basic meaning of grace is that God has done something for us that he did not have to do and that we did not have coming to us in the contract. Something has happened that alters life radically for the better. Until we are in the new state, we did not know how badly off we were before. Therefore, we have not found the new by deliberately planning and changing our ways. Instead, finding ourselves in the new condition, we have felt ourselves drawn to this by a benevolent power not our own.[2]

When God's grace is being recognized, therefore, the human sign of acknowledgment is, at first, a kind of ejaculation, "Thanks be unto God who. . . ." The human acknowledgment and feeling is similar to freedom in the dimension of release from bondage. But what is emphasized there is release, while in the foreground here is thankfulness. At this stage, there is mainly feeling and not much reflection: honest thankfulness. We did not deserve it but here it is.

When such an acknowledgment is felt and honest thanks are rendered to God, then the immediate perceptual effect is to focus attention upon the gracious character and work of God rather than upon the self. Such an act is thoroughly logical. But in practice it has often meant a reluctance to analyze the quality of thankfulness, so that, after the height of the experience had passed, there would remain only ritualistic statements about God's grace, and no permanent effect upon one's capacity for thankfulness.

In the New Testament grace is represented both as the loving and merciful action of God in Jesus Christ that has rescued and saved man, and also as the continuing guidance and support that enables man to go on in his new life. Thus grace came from one unified God. But in accord with the doctrine of the Trinity that was systematized later, grace was especially associated with Jesus Christ in terms of the means of salvation already carried out, and with the Holy Spirit as continuing guide and support. The New Testament mood about grace is "eucharistic." In this word the root *charis* or grace is joined by the prefix *eu* meaning positive or favorable. As even the English language retains, the "eucharist" became the principal term for the central act of Christian worship, showing how central was the feeling about expressing deep thankfulness.

As usually happens with core theological ideas, this one also began in a glow and later required a more analytical and less ecstatic look. From the second and third centuries onward, the church fathers asked probing questions about grace and were unsatisfied with the notion of the glow. For instance, if grace is all God's doing, and man is utterly unworthy to participate in it, then how does he receive it at all?

Augustine, in the fourth century, had a neat little bypass around this dilemma. He asserted that the desire for the help of grace is the beginning of the operation of grace.[3] To others like his opponent Pelagius, this seemed like an evasive reply. If man ever does receive grace, must he not have some kind of grace-receiving potential? Perhaps God often tries and cannot get through. But if he has given man some real freedom and not made him a robot, there must be something in human beings that is a potential receiver when grace is being broadcast.

We do well to recognize what was at stake in these early theological discussions of grace. On the one side, it was unthinkable that man should be able to push buttons, even the buttons of the eucharist, and thereby make God's grace go into action as if it had been lying in wait for the bell. Indeed, if button-pressing would work, God would be neither a just nor a loving God, and the man who pressed the buttons would not be worshiping but engaged in magic. So it was clear that the grace of God had to be seen as operating, so to speak, exclusively from the will of God. At that time men did not have an intellectual apparatus to protect this all-important point about grace coming from God alone, and yet to show, at the same time, the presence of some kind of receptors that could properly, according to Augustine's intuition, be altered by a strong human desire. So the discussions were in terms that seem paradoxical today.

At many times in the history of the church there was also the question as to why special grace from God was needed. Was there not something like general grace and favor of mankind in the creation itself? In raising these questions and speaking to them, Christians were much influenced by the history of the Jewish people, in which the people had to be rescued many times by new measures after their backslidings. Christians were also affected by reflection on their own individual and corporate lives. Even though they believed themselves to have been saved by Jesus Christ, they knew and admitted backslidings of many kinds. When they came to themselves and realized what was happening, they were right, in a psychological sense, to believe that something new had been added, even though it was their own blindness, and not God's intention, that had to be changed to get them to wake up.

The doctrine of grace, therefore, is a declaration that God is involved with the movement and progress of what he has created, and does not stand aloofly above or aside from his creation. He parted the waters of the Red Sea so the Jews could get through, and he sent his only begotten Son so that men could be saved. Reflection showed that God's intent for mankind did not change, but he was prepared to use extraordinary measures (so long as they did not violate man's freedom) to extricate men from their dilemmas. To recognize that God is gracious is, therefore, not only to acknowledge some unexpected and benevolent part of his action. It is also, in a more general sense, to admit thankfully that he is aware of and in-

41

volved in the present human condition no matter what its nature.

From the point of view of grace as a special act of favor or love on God's part, therefore, the critical declaration is that God, in love and benevolence but still respecting man's freedom, is deeply immersed in his creation. From the point of view of man's response to grace, the main point stressed was that man should be thankful. True, thankfulness was dealt with in a more hortatory than analytical way. It was often presented as a duty, lest man take its benefits for granted and say "So what" instead of thanks. Man was also warned that he should have some better criterion for thankfulness than whether he got what he wanted.

Grace, then, is a doctrine not only about God's love and benevolence, but also about his involvement with mankind. Implicit in the teaching is a lure toward the appropriate human response once the reality of grace is recognized. This ought to be genuine thankfulness, as we agree today. But since the idea was not analyzed in human terms, it often slipped away. So it tends to do even today. Hence our concentration on an analysis of gratitude.[4]

Some Fights About Grace

In the early Christian understanding of freedom as release from bondage, there was some reflection. But it became serious only when freedom as self-direction was also considered. In a similar way, grace was initially evocative of thankfulness mainly in an emotive sense. But deeper reflection came when disagreements arose and led to controversy.

In the fight between Augustine and Pelagius in the fourth century about questions like grace and freedom, the issue was not whether all grace and favor come from God. The disputants agreed on that point. As they saw the question, it was whether man retained a residue of receptivity to grace. Pelagius, who had an eclectic common sense, thought that man did have some such receptivity. Apparently more illogical, Augustine said no, even though he admitted that the desire for grace might open us to the beginning of its work in our lives.

Nearly all serious later opinion has sided with Augustine on this point.[5] Paradoxical as his answer was, he designed it to prevent any notion that grace was a power that man could use for his own ends (which were likely to be wrong due to sin and the abuse of freedom). Dynamically speaking, the merit in Augustine's position was something like this: If you can influence it, then you do not have to be thankful for it, and in the absence of thankfulness, grace tends to disappear. Nevertheless, I believe that Pelagius was short-changed by history. He was not a believer in simple voluntarism. If he were around today, I think I might get along with him better than with Augustine, even though I should have to point out to him some modern psychological findings that tend to support Augustine's paradoxical position about freedom and grace.

All through Christian history and the humanism that has accompanied it, there has been the question most sharply stated by Voltaire: God forgives us because that is his *métier*.[6] If it is God's "job" to forgive, then the last feeling one will have is gratitude or thankfulness. My own opinion is that Voltaire's question is logical and not irreligious, but that he posed it out of neutral feelings rather than out of feelings of gratitude. In other words, what Voltaire did not take seriously was not so much God as gratitude.

A protracted fight about grace was whether it is irresistible or only prevenient. Certainly grace "comes before," as the Latin meaning of "prevenient" indicates. We view its work only retrospectively, after it has done something for and to us. But is it irresistible as well as prevenient?[7] If God makes up his mind to change the most resistive of sinners, does this happen? The people who declared grace to be irresistible were trying to assure that grace would be thought of as coming wholly from God and his will. Yet the very notion of God's deciding to change this sinner implied his deciding not to reach that one, so that the world of irresistible grace came very close to being populated by robots. Furthermore, most of the proponents were reasonably sure that they were included in the divine favor.

The prevenience of grace is, however, quite another kind of

matter and of permanent significance. Even at a secular level where the theological concept of grace would not be understood, it is nevertheless something very much like grace that often operates with saving effect. I think, for instance, of an intelligent psychiatric patient who had a long and difficult time receiving multiple forms of therapy. Although he was incapacitated for some periods, he was able to proceed with his therapy for part time over six or seven years, and was then able to resume his work and relationships. After he was back at his job I asked him what had been the principal contribution of his main therapist over the years. He replied, "He believed in me when I didn't believe in myself." This statement is an acknowledgment of a secular version of prevenient grace.

The last controversy about grace that will be mentioned is that which arose between Catholics and Protestants centuries ago. Whether rightly or wrongly, Protestants charged that Catholics were using the sacraments with people, giving them or withholding them, as if there were something automatic in the way they made God's grace available. To early Protestant sensibilities, such procedures seemed like a kind of button pushing, made worse because it had obvious social consequences in keeping people tied to the Catholic Church. Probably there was Protestant excess in such charges. And many of the practices of which Protestants complained were soon cleaned up by Catholics. I still think that Protestants were right about the principle that, if grace seems to be controlled by anything human, person or institution, its fundamental meaning is lost. But it is dubious that Catholics were so heinous as the early Protestants believed.

In order to try to set in perspective what grace is really about, let us examine a bit of fiction—the successive reflections of someone who has actually experienced something like grace in his life experience.

1. *This is a magnificent day! I had no idea that such a gift even existed. And even if I had, I should never have thought that it would come my way. I did not order it, did not expect it, and I have done nothing to deserve it. But here it is, in its wonderful concreteness. And thank God for it!*

2. *It is marvelous to use the new gift, which helps everything, fits everything, satisfies everything, and does something for my stance in life that nothing else has ever done.*

3. *The gift certainly is wonderful. But now that I have it, I am aware that some other people have it also. So it does not make me a member of the spiritual country club as I had first thought. Still, it's great.*

4. *If the donor has so many of these things available, he must have been able to see that I needed it long before he sent it. I wonder why he waited? I don't like to think of all those years when I might have had it and didn't.*

5. *If this great product has been around for some time and I didn't know it, I wonder if there are not other even more miraculous things available, lying around somewhere if only one could get at them.*

6. *Now that I see what this is really like, I guess I have been a bit over-grateful to the donor. At least up to a point, I think I might have made it myself.*

From this point onward the sequence might go in either of two ways. The first would be a return to honest thankfulness, and the second, on to suspicion, arrogance, resentment, or envy. In other words, it is very difficult to maintain an appropriate response to grace. Once bestowed and received, it becomes a part of the way things are, and there are great temptations to take its benefits for granted.

Dynamics of Gratitude

The Lithuanian word *ačiū* has reminded us that language itself has often recognized the difference between conventional and serious gratitude. As the discussion will attempt to move toward understanding the dynamics of genuine gratitude, it will deal with phenomena that look like genuine gratitude but are actually something else.

The first pattern to be noted may be called "reactive gratitude." It reacts to a situation of danger from which one has escaped, but it tends to be short-lived. We may think, for example, of a wealthy patient whose illness is serious. He appeals to the surgeon to do everything possible for him. Cost is no object, and he may even hint that the hospital might get a new wing if he comes through. Then comes the surgery. And along with the pain there is the verdict that the patient will recover. At that point the grateful comments made to the surgeon and others are likely to be strong and even effusive. He may even say, "When I get home, I will do something for your hospital." But day by day the expressions of thanks, while not absent, grow less vivid. Unless the surgeon gets the patient's signature on the dotted line before he leaves the hospital, it is unlikely that there will be a new wing. At home a month later, the patient may even growl about the amount of the surgeon's charges.

Also in illustrating temporary reactive gratitude, we may think of a man in a business organization who is called one day into the office of the big boss and informed that he is to have a certain coveted privilege, something the man himself had not dared to hope for. After recovering from his immediate disbelief, his initial reaction is likely to be, "I can't tell you how much I appreciate your letting me in on this." But later, after he has talked the matter over thoroughly with his wife, and perhaps received congratulations from fellow workers, his private musings are likely to swing in the direction of, "I wonder what scheme he really has up his sleeve?"

The beginning of getting at the dynamics of such situations may be found in the comment of Oscar Wilde about a certain man. Wilde said that he did not know why the man hated him because he, Wilde, had never done anything for the man.[8]

The possibility of genuine gratitude is present only when what has been done for us is truly important to us, and when the other person was not under compulsion to do what he did. But people who have the ability to do something sterling for us have, thereby, a kind of power in relation to us. What happens in reactive gratitude is that, for a time, we forget the power and enjoy the gift. But when the gift has been around a while and seems less strange, then we begin to react, perhaps unconsciously, against the power that the other held over us, even though he has used it benevolently. Even with a good and needed gift, the power of the other to give it reminds us of our dependency. In psychiatric terms, this situation reactivates our infantile sense of helplessness and our resentment over it. So what began as reactive and genuine thanks, and concentration on the gift, tends to be short-lived. What will happen later depends on many kinds of factors in the person, the situation, and the giver. But it seems likely that most human gratitude is of this brief reactive type.

Closely related to reactive gratitude in its dynamics, but more pathological in nature and result, is what may be termed pseudo-gratitude. In such situations expressions of thanks, which are sometimes effusive, are actually used to divert attention, of the self or the others, away from where it ought to be. Freud in his early work sensed that pseudo-gratitude on the part of patients could divert them from working on their real problems, and he believed that one way to prevent this was in requiring the patients to pay fees. Although many other factors are involved in the question of fees, Freud's insight still seems significant so far as it goes.

We can find striking instances of the subversive effect of pseudo-gratitude in many alcoholic patients including those in Alcoholics Anonymous. Here is a patient, for example, who had for some time told A. A. members that he could handle his problem himself. They assured him that he could not, but that they would be available if he changed his mind. After getting himself into the worst jam of all, he called them, and they helped him without saying, "We told you so." His next move, however, was to thank them effusively for their help. They, on the other hand, while accepting his conscious intentions, nevertheless said to him in effect, "Look, don't be grateful to us. We are still working out the problems of our own lives by helping you. Put your mind on your own problem." In such instances, pseudo-gratitude may be a defensive diversion away from the problem that needs to be confronted.

As a teacher I have learned to be suspicious of a student whose gratitude seems overdone in relation to my help in planning a paper or project. It is unlikely to be conscious strategy on his part, but in giving me all the thanks he may be drawing up a kind of hidden contract as if to say, "Since I appreciate your help so much, you will of course appreciate my paper more when you get it, and therefore give it a higher grade."

The difference between reactive gratitude and pseudo-gratitude is real. The former begins with quite honest feelings, and with concentration upon the gift that has been made available. Only later does it tend to feel resentful about the power of the giver, and thus to depreciate the gift. Pseudo-gratitude, from the beginning, is a dynamic strategy of concealment, even though the strategy is rarely conscious and deliberate. Reactive gratitude always has some chance of becoming genuine gratitude if the issues about power and resentment can be dealt with honestly. On the contrary, pseudo-gratitude has no such potential since its apparent thanks are only defense strategies.

We turn next to the category of genuine gratitude. The previous discussions of reactive gratitude and pseudo-gratitude are good introductions, in that they tell us what not to look for. From pseudo-gratitude we see that genuine gratitude cannot be present if the primary motivation is of a defensive and concealing sort. From reactive gratitude we see that genuine gratitude must work through its problems about resentment of the donor's power, and not attempt to deny or hide them or simply yield to them. Further, genuine gratitude needs to be lasting.

If we look for genuine gratitude first in more intimate personal kinds of relationships, such as marriage, the most obvious fact is that, even when it is most marked, gratitude is never pure. A husband, for instance, has fortunately remembered the date of his wife's birthday and brought her some flowers. She really means it when she thanks him, kisses him warmly, but does not get effusive. But at the same time, knowing him, she recognizes that it was fifty-fifty whether he would remember, and that, if he had not, she would have felt hurt even if she did not say so. Genuine as her feeling of gratitude is now. some part of her resents the fact that she is so attached in the marriage relationship as to be dependent upon a fallible connubial memory. This latter fact does not mean that she lacks genuine gratitude. It simply means that even genuine human gratitude is never pure and unmixed.

In the sexual relationships of a long-married couple, even if they have troubles and problems, we can often see signs of genuine gratitude, even though the verbal expressions may be brief and partly inverted. Whatever the troubles, something happens in this long-term relationship which, while it may not have the excitement of novelty, nevertheless provides an unexpected gift of a different kind. The capacity for wonder is kept alive, and the gratitude is real. Here also, however, grateful feelings are not unmixed with others. Perhaps the husband wrote out a check for a new rug the morning after last week. What human wife is not tempted next week to relate sex and the draperies she also wants?

Some observers believe that, except for small children, real gratitude may be a disappearing factor in parent-child relationships, especially with growing affluence and the teen-age culture tending to believe it has a right to whatever is available. Even if this is true, it is not clear that it is wholly a bad development. Many teen-agers are sensitive to the falsity of pseudo-gratitude among their elders, and that is good so far as it goes. Further, I suspect that adult society has long tried to evoke gratitude from its adolescents basically as a means of keeping them under control by acknowledging their power. Adolescent attempts not to feel grateful, therefore, can be stimuli to a new kind of self-responsibility. Whether they will become so, or will simply drift into contempt for whatever has gone before, remains still to be seen.

When we look at small children, genuine gratitude seems most apparent no matter how short-lived it is. Recently a four-year-old showed me a fistful of a dozen pennies or so. His grandfather gave it to him he said, for carrying some logs into the house. He had earned it, and therefore he did not have to thank grandpa. But I believe he had some brief grateful feelings nevertheless. He felt needed and important, and grandpa had helped him to feel so. Small children, with their short span of attention, remind us that even the most genuine gratitude is begun in brevity, and that part of the dynamic we are searching for is to see how thankfulness can be sustained beyond the time span in which we have all learned it if we have learned it at all.

When we move beyond intimate relationships of family and close friendship into the other kinds of interpersonal and person-institution relationships, it becomes even more difficult to identify genuine gratitude and to separate it from pseudo-gratitude and reactive gratitude. A successful political candidate, even if he makes good on all his campaign promises, is likely to have only a short honeymoon of reactive gratitude with the voters before that begins to be balanced by resentment and disappointment. A man out of work is temporarily grateful when he gets a good job. But in a short while he is likely to believe that his employer was simply shrewd enough to see his genuine merits.

Even more obviously than in intimate relationships, genuine gratitude in less personal forms of contact is likely to be mixed with something else, and if the something else is not massive, it does not destroy the gratitude. Some of the sharpest critics of evils in our national life, for instance, may nevertheless be most deeply grateful for the benefits that our heritage has brought. Realistic patriotism devoid of chauvinism is itself a form of gratitude to forefathers.

Our society traditionally expected gratitude from all kinds of less privileged people, just as parents tended to expect it from children. Servants, the poor, the sick, the uneducated, and many others were expected to be grateful for what society, or one of its agents, did to help them in their condition. It is plain today that most such groups resent very much the expectation that they should be grateful. They believe they have rights; they are developing powers to support the rights, and when they make progress, the last feeling they want to have is gratitude for what somebody else did for them.

So long as it does not lead to violence, who can deny that there is soundness in this "relief from imposed gratitude obligations"? The present situation, with its renunciation of obligations to be grateful, makes it clear that a great deal of the gratitude previously inculcated into servants, children, the poor, the workers, and others was simply an indoctrination into the benevolence of the powerful. So long as that persisted or persists (it is not yet dead), ordinary men are quite likely, beyond the family circle, to reject feelings of gratitude altogether.

For the most part, therefore, I believe that our society today is in a kind of "moratorium on gratitude" period. In a Black man, gratitude looks like Uncle Tom. In a teen-ager, it looks like middle-class conventionalism. In a worker, it looks like denial of his own rights. And in women, it looks increasingly like an acceptance of the male-dominated status quo.

In a general sense, I believe that the increasing freedom from "imposed obligations to gratitude" is excellent. The world is far better off without slaves compelled to be grateful to their masters. Thus, I believe that all the movements that have been cited, and many others as well, that reject any obligation for imposed gratitude, are themselves necessary steps in getting rid of the exploitative use of gratitude that has characterized so much of the human past. Coerced gratitude is not gratitude at all. It is a form of pseudo-gratitude, achieving its form not through the individual psychodynamics discussed previously but through cultural conditioning of the powerless by the powerful. To make real strides in getting rid of such nonsense is, among other things, to reopen the way to genuine gratitude.

It is interesting to speculate—my knowledge permits nothing more—about what is happening to gratitude in Communist countries. All along there has been much "imposed obligation to gratitude," always with the attempt to indoctrinate the person so that he believes this is his real and sole attitude. Studies of Communist brainwashing suggest that the final mark of success there is gratitude.[9] Communist leaders everywhere, however, are not so naïve as to rely on imposed gratitude as a major force. They provide, or talk about providing, more consumer goods. They improve their technologies and forget their ideologies when a foreign trade plan looks good. Nevertheless, in striking imitation of older kings and czars, they tend to crack down on those who are not grateful for what the regime has brought and produced. If Communists ever move in the

51

direction of freedom as we know it in the West, it is possible that the first signs will be their renunciation of an obligation to be grateful to the state, to Marx or Lenin, or to the system.

Fortunately, we are not in a lockstep system. We are very much in process of getting rid of the imposed obligations to gratitude, however slowly some aspects of the process seem to move. For a moment at least, let us assume that all these old impositions will be done away with in reasonable time. What, then, will happen to gratitude? No longer demanded, will it die altogether? Or, outside the family, will it remain suspended in a kind of paranoid suspicion? Or will it get a new and authentic lease on life precisely because the old compulsory modes of gratitude are dead?

My conviction remains that we are currently in an "interim" or "moratorium" period about gratitude. Being against gratitude right now may be a friend, rather than an enemy, of authentic gratitude to emerge later. A very great deal of gratitude in the past has been enforced, either externally as by kings to servants or masters to slaves, or internally, as by modern Communists. But gratitude in its essence cannot be forced. If it is not spontaneous, it is not gratitude at all. We must, therefore, reject all forms of imposed gratitude obligations, even when they are made in the name of God. To put all this in more traditional language, the end does not necessarily justify the means. The means also have to be investigated.

At least in terms of personal types of relationship, it should be possible some day to construct a test which, at least in a rough form, could yield "genuine gratitude quotient" scores. This assumption is based on the belief that the capacity for gratitude is not simply a mark of the situation or a function of the value of the gift, but that it is also related to character. We no longer use the old term "ingrate." But at least in a relative sense, people probably belong on a continuum line between "ingrate" and "grate."

Since the person with capacity for genuine gratitude must, somewhere along the line, accept the fact that the donor has a kind of power and that one is therefore in some respects dependent, one mark of ability to be grateful would be coming to terms with authority figures. And yet, apart from extreme positions such as defiance or genuflection, it is not easy to make appraisals about relationship to authority figures.

It seems also probably true that capacity for gratitude is higher in persons who have more of what is called ego-strength, an important idea however difficult to define. Common sense suggests that the reverse is clearly true, that persons with low ego-strength are more likely to resort to pseudo-gratitude or no gratitude at all. And yet sometimes ego-strength is bought at the price of some personal and social sensitivity. In all probability, ego-strength is an ingredient in ability to be genuinely grateful but would certainly not guarantee that result.

As the previous paragraph has already begun to suggest, a factor of sensitivity must also be involved in the capacity for genuine gratitude. Whatever this is, it must be very complex. For it is plain that a person who simply needs other people or things would not necessarily qualify. And one who is elated by a gift only because he would be hurt without it would not score high either. For a deeper understanding of gratitude, I believe that just such complex factors will have to be investigated.

So far our discussion of gratitude and its deviations has assumed the person as receiving a gift. There is the other side as well, receiving responses from others when we have given them a gift. I am convinced that the capacity to receive thanks, when deserved, and to give them are closely related.

Nothing is more familiar to us in professional work than a situation in which we rendered honestly felt praise to a colleague for what he had done, and found him unable to receive it. In less extreme form there are people who can only joke about praise or a compliment. There are of course others for whom nothing we can say in praise is adequate. For those who are unable at all to accept praise or thanks, my observation is that they tend to be people who cannot comfortably associate themselves with any kind of power or authority. To acknowledge that they have it would create a kind of responsibility they are unprepared to face. So if the gift can be ignored or belittled, they can maintain the psychological status quo.

THEOLOGICAL DYNAMICS

Although this discussion makes a bare beginning at understanding the dynamics of gratitude, I hope that it will stimulate more study and reflection. Very little study or work has been done on gratitude.

Grace and Gratitude

Theology declares that God works graciously and not merely by a conception of original rules, that he is benevolently involved in human life at all times, and that the appropriate human response to God's extra gifts is gratitude. Our human task is to recognize the gifts when they come and to be as genuinely grateful for them as we can.

It is, therefore, impossible to understand grace theologically unless attention is also given to gratitude.[10] Better understanding of the dynamics of gratitude will, therefore, be of direct relevance to a theology of grace. In addition to improved theoretical understanding of the dynamics of gratitude, or its absence, it seems potentially possible for psychiatrists and their colleagues to increase the capacity for gratitude in some persons. Although such an achievement would not carry over automatically into the theology of grace, it would be a move in that direction.

A full teaching about grace in any particular theology would have some specifics of content that have been ignored in the present discussion. But a theology of grace priding itself only on its unique content, and failing to recognize its necessary similarity to genuine gratitude understood at the psychological level, would be a kind of abstraction ignoring the very bases upon which proper human responsiveness to God's grace must be built.

Chapter 3
PROVIDENCE AND TRUST

Very few theological doctrines regarded as significant in the past have been so little spoken of in modern times as God's providence. Two reasons have contributed to this neglect. The first was the consequence of a serious error in Protestant theological history during the sixteenth and seventeenth centuries.

At that time, especially in Calvinism though not in Calvin, God's providence became associated with a kind of predestinarian teaching so extreme as virtually to cancel out the human freedom that God gave in creating man.[1] Under the double predestination teaching (with some saved in advance and others damned), it was possible to think of God as watching a tiny baby and assigning it to a destination in hell. To be sure, the motive behind such teaching was intended to be the protection of God's complete sovereignty over human affairs. But later ages became more humane and were wary of any doctrine that could be interpreted to have such a meaning. As I shall indicate later, I believe the whole context of the predestination discussion distorted the real significance of the teaching about God's providence.

The other reason for neglect of the providence doctrine is more modern. When providence, quite apart from the cosmological predestination context, was set forth as God's literally taking care, hour after hour, of every bird and beast and man, then the logical conclusion to draw from this situation was that we ourselves could and should do nothing. Of course such a conclusion was not actually drawn. No interpreter was so rash as to plunge headlong into a chasm while trusting in God, or to believe that God alone would take care of everything about church attendance. And insofar as Protestant theology became sophisticated, the tension of the paradox was always maintained. But in much popular preaching, especially in America, providence became associated with God's looking after every detail, even though the people who held that view were anything but passive in their approach to life. In reaction to a doctrine so one-sidedly interpreted, theologians came in our own century to say little about providence at all.

There are some recent signs, as in the book by Albert C. Outler, that the doctrine of providence may be in for a revival.[2] I hope so, for I believe the real intent of this teaching is crucial for theological understanding in all times, and perhaps especially so in our own. There is a significant sense in which the grasp of providence in its proper meaning is the most important thing that can be said about God.[3] For the question that the doctrine tries to answer is: How is God involved in our lives at all times? Since the doctrine of creation refers not only to how things got started but also goes on to how they are maintained, one may even argue that the dynamic dimension of the doctrine of creation is capable of being subsumed under the teaching about God's providence. And if the principal evidence of God's providence is what he did in Jesus Christ, then Christology retains its appropriately paramount place in Christian thought, but the providence of God is not confined to what he did in and through Jesus Christ. To a degree, then, even Christology may be seen as the principal part of the doctrine of providence but not exhausting it.

A special reason for refurbishing this teaching in our time is related to what have been called the "secular" tendencies in contemporary theology, with special reference to the kind of thinking that Dietrich Bonhoeffer did.[4] Bonhoeffer believed that the whole purpose of faith is distorted or destroyed if we try to call on God to do things for us that we can do, or can learn to do, for ourselves. The achievements of modern science and technology, and their even greater promise for the future, make it inevitable that prayers for rain without serious efforts at weather control, or bewailing cancer but having no research on it, are doomed. Thus, many of the old standby ways in which God's providential care has been represented are either dated or dead. Whatever interpretations are given now must be both honest and subtle, coming face to face with the paradox (but not contradiction) of God's guidance and man's creative abilities. If the teaching cannot be so restated, it will die, and with it what is perhaps the most basic understanding we may have about God, namely, how he is constantly related to his creation.

An Introduction on Terms

Our word "providence" comes directly from the Latin *provideo*. The term "providence" itself was not used in the Bible, but Hebrew and Greek equivalents of *provideo* were used. All these terms meant simply to supply, to furnish, or to make available.

One does not have to be a language expert to see, however, that the root meaning of *provideo* is to "see before" or to "see ahead." The same is true of the cognate Greek word *pronoia*. The etymological question is, then: How could words that originally meant "see ahead" come automatically to take on the meaning of "supply" or "furnish"?

The one way in which we can regard this movement as a natural progression is to assume that, in the nature or character of the one who is seeing ahead, there is a kind of benevolence which, if it sees a need, moves to meet it. If the one who looks ahead were of divided mind, then he might see a need but be too tired or too weak or too double-minded to make the effort to meet it. In the actual development of the meaning of these words in the ancient languages, therefore, there is testimony to the automatic relationship between seeing ahead and supplying; and therefore to the unambiguous benevolence of the one who sees ahead.

From the point of view of social history, it is probably true that this conjunction between the two meanings of *provideo* (seeing ahead and supplying) was influenced by the Oriental conceptions of hospitality where it was mandatory to take care of the traveler who, otherwise, would be dead in harsh desert lands.

In one of its most poignant forms we see the connection between seeing ahead and supplying in the New Testament story of the father and his prodigal son.[5] When he had reached the end of his rope, the son began his return home. His father saw him while he was still some distance away, gave orders for a banquet, and then went out to meet him. This story by Jesus is of course about God, not about a human father. And it is striking how seeing ahead and supplying are linked by the central point of the story, namely, the unambiguously benevolent character of God.

If the development of language in this instance can be trusted, therefore, the initial problem to be posed is whether God is, in fact, unambiguously for his creation and especially human beings. Our forefathers were certainly not ignorant of events and realities (e.g., natural disasters, illness, premature death, insufficient food) that might be interpreted otherwise. We do need to ask first, then, the question of whether the assumption behind the movement from seeing ahead to supplying is mere wishful thinking, or a realistic picture of God.[6] If we establish the point, then the question following immediately is: What is the relation between what we can supply ourselves and what God supplies because only he can do it?

The forms (case histories of a kind) in which God's providential supplying were shown have been a combination of crudity and sophistication, beginning with the Bible. Even the crude stories, however, like that of God's raining down manna when the people would otherwise have starved, must be understood as making the supplying relevant to the actuality of the need.[7] There was no artificial separation of religious or spiritual need from general human need.

Needs and Wants

The preliminary word analysis has shown that teaching about providence involves three basic assumptions. First, there is God's clearly benevolent attention to and intention for mankind. Second, there is God's looking ahead to see what man needs that he, unaided, will not be able to supply for himself.

Third, there is the action on God's part to supply what mankind needs and cannot provide for itself.

Since the world contains sin and evil as well as God's benevolence, the first implication of the above points is that God must make a distinction between what man really needs and what he may want to his own detriment. Therefore, even from the first some kind of distinction had to be made by men between genuine needs and other kinds of desires or wants. Once such a process has begun, then the method or the criteria of making the distinctions may be the critical factors. For, once this stage of reflection has been reached, it is plain that the reality of God's providential guidance cannot be tested by merely indicating whether he gave you what you asked for. Thus, some discipline of self-criticism was built in from the very beginning.

In modern disciplines involving child care, psychiatry, psychology, social work, and others, the initial impulse was to do away altogether with the distinction between needs and wants. Not all wants could be accepted at face value. The destructive child could not be helped merely by encouraging or permitting his destructiveness. But beneath his ineffective and self-defeating methods, it was held that he was attempting to gain something that he really needed. It was the task of would-be helpers, therefore, to see and acknowledge those underlying needs and to help him to move toward their realization by better means than he had come upon spontaneously. Thus, some genuine needs were held to be present beneath even the most arbitrary or antisocial wants.

Especially in the light of many developments in modern youth culture, this general picture of the relationship between needs and wants has had hard sledding. A graphic illustration of this reversion was seen recently in the parents of many students at Kent State University in Ohio who, even if their own student children were not extremists or revolutionaries, wanted all students to "shape up," sometimes regarding bare feet, long hair, disinclinations to bathe, and odd costumes to be warrant for National Guard bullets.[8] In less extreme form, many people in our society prejudge negatively everything about the culture of our modern youth as containing only irresponsible desires and wanton wishes, and deny that beneath the often unhappy form of youthful rebellion there may be something resembling a genuine need.

Nevertheless, even the most ardent advocates of the notion that wants always reveal needs, even if they sometimes conceal them, have come to see that the earlier position was too simpleminded. Some means of expressing wants are so inherently self-defeating that, even if genuine needs are hidden beneath them, attention must be given first to some changing of the behavior and the wants before the needs can be approached. However fallibly, our society must make judgments about the kinds of want-fulfillment that are inherently self-defeating, and the others, so that a pragmatic distinction is always made between wants that obscure or threaten the meeting of needs, and wants that can be reformed methodologically into the real needs.

Society can never move entirely beyond the effort to make some kind of proper distinction between needs and wants. But it can try to avoid the making of snap judgments about the relationship of needs and wants. There should always be some tension. If this group carries out this behavior, basically in order to meet these legitimate needs, when does the behavior itself not only harm society but also tend to defeat the meeting of the basic needs? Not infrequently, a sober appraisal based on this criterion will differ from general judgments.

Modern psychiatry and the disciplines related to it understand human motivations as appearing at different levels, with all kinds of complexities, and with a single-level conception of motivation as seldom true to the facts.[9] This discovery will prove, in our subsequent discussion, to be important for understanding in dynamic fashion the providence of God.

Closely related to the self-criticism that tried to distinguish between real needs and desires or wants, in the Bible and later, was the conviction about the kinds of supplies that God holds uniquely as against those that man can stockpile for himself. In the biblical accounts, God is shown as having two general kinds of supplies. First, there are those needed in response to particular situations: manna in the desert, freedom from captivity through traversing the Red Sea, and above all Jesus Christ, who also met the needs of future as well as present generations. Second, God is shown as having permanently the kinds of supplies that men cannot produce for themselves, whether understood as revelation, grace, the gift of faith, or in other ways. All these concepts imply that man, left to himself, would overlook the most important factors in the situation. Hence, they provide him with needed clues to understand properly where he really is. It is important to recognize that, from earliest days, a self-critical principle came into operation about God's providential action, both at the human and the divine levels.[10]

The self-critical principle is of course not unique to the West, even though it has taken different forms in the East where the attempted elimination of wants rather than shaping them has been the trend. Every culture has some ironic equivalent of the three wishes. A man is granted, by some power, three special wishes. He uses up the first on an impulse about something trivial. Then his wife, for instance, criticizes his choice, and he uses up his second wish in getting back at her. She then complains so fiercely about whatever has happened to her, such as an elongated nose, that the final wish must be used to restore her to her previous condition. In none of these stories has anyone ever wished for a permanently filled deep-freeze, for eternal youth, or for wisdom. Thus, the general assessment of human motivation, East and West, has shown a great deal of realism, even sometimes to the point of cynicism. Whatever might be man's needs, he is the last to know how they can be met even when he receives special powers.

The preliminary analysis shows, therefore, that we must respect and study the difference between needs and wants, that we must not make a categorical distinction between them, but that we must make distinctions based on the probability of outcome of this or that kind of movement in behavior as it may or may not help or hinder the meeting of genuine needs.

The basic position from which we move is that providence must always involve some basic kind of trust in a God who is already for us in a way that we cannot be for ourselves, who looks ahead of us and sees our needs as we cannot do, and who has supplies to meet the needs we cannot meet for ourselves. Nevertheless, even the critical decision about whether a need is genuine or not is a part of our own responsibility.

The Biblical Paradigm About Providence

From Karl Barth, with whom I have disagreed on many matters, I have gained much of my understanding of providence as adumbrated in the Bible.[11] What follows is my own interpretation of the story of Lot and his family in the Old Testament. But the clue to this story, and why it is such a remarkable paradigm about God's providence, came from Barth.

In the story Lot, who is a good man, is being led, along with his family, out of the wicked city of Sodom by the angels.[12] The city has been slated as a redevelopment area by the Lord, and the ancient equivalent of bulldozers is about to move in. On divine instruction, the angelic guides chart out the route that the Lot family is to take, leading them to the hills and to safety. But at this point, on the outskirts of Sodom, Lot insists on dialogic communication with the angels. He says he does not want to go to the hills, but wishes instead to go in another direction to the little city of Zoar. He said he was afraid he would die if he went to the hills. Perhaps he had learned, even in the evil city of Sodom, to relish aspects of urban life, and dreaded the prospect of being too far in the country.

At any rate, the angels immediately grant Lot's request. He is free to head for Zoar instead of the hills. For the intent of the story, we must assume that the angels are not simply being appeased, or that they are ignorant of the advantages of either spot. The angels do not chide Lot for daring to question the precise route selected by God. They accept his obedience at the point where it counts, namely, getting out of Sodom and heading to another sensible spot. That fact seems important to them, whereas the precise route, even though they have had previous instructions about it, seems secondary. In being attentive to God's providence, Lot does not have to lose his own ideas.

At this point in the story emerges the element of family complication. They are just outside Sodom and have completed the route-planning conference with the angels. Then they hear, behind them, the fire and brimstone at work that will shortly destroy the city. The angels warn them strongly not to look back. Lot and his daughters follow this advice. But Mrs. Lot cannot resist; she turns and looks back, and she is then turned into a pillar of salt. Lot may have been sad enough, but the biblical story reports no comment from him on this event. He was not accountable for this particular action on the part of his wife. Perhaps, a modern interpretation suggests, he may have been relieved at liberation from a gossipy mate who must always have had to see and hear everything.

Barth has an interesting comment on the looking back. There is always, he notes, some kind of fire behind us. The injunction not to look back is not to try to have us be ignorant of this fact or, as we would say in modern language, to repress the fact. But if we are attentive to God's providence and trust in his leading, then what we shall be relieved from is compulsion to look back, i.e., to be preoccupied with the past. The focus of perception is on the steps to the future, even in the dire circumstance in which one's spouse has turned to sodium chloride.

The story of the Lot family shows that there is a negative as well as a positive aspect to providence in its meaning of seeing ahead. Providence is, by analogy, both the radar that looks ahead to warn of obstacles and the beacon that guides toward a destination. We get some linguistic hint of this connection in the English conjunction "provided," meaning "conditional upon." In any event, the story makes it clear that providence is very far from depriving us of choices. As subsequent events show, Lot may have made a poor choice.[13] Later on, the story shows his daughters, despairing about not having husbands who could help them to have children, getting their father drunk so that they could have sexual relations with him, become pregnant, and remedy the deficiency. But the Bible tells

63

its history forward and not backward. There is no later moralizing to suggest that, at the gates of Sodom, Lot should have followed the angelic advice in detail.

There is a final point about providence suggested by the story of Lot. This has to do with scarcity. It may well be that, until affairs in Sodom reached the critical point, Lot had taken angelic care for granted. But when the crisis came, the angels moved in and got the Lot family out of Sodom. With the exception of Mrs. Lot and her fatal accident en route, the Lot family would have been more attentive to providential guidance after they had been through the rescue experience than before.

From this event in the paradigm there emerges a point about the relationship between general and special needs that will be important in the later discussion of trust. Before the crisis, Lot had general trust in the Lord. Indeed, that fact is shown, in the story, to be why Lot and his family were led out of the city and others were not. But it took the special crisis experience, and release from it, to show Lot what trust really meant and why God was providential. From then on, the special experience would leave an indelible mark upon all subsequent experiences. In the time of scarcity or special need, Lot found God giving special support. Lot would remember that the Lord is sufficient unto the specialty of need.

Dynamics of Trust

Thanks especially to Erik Erikson, trust has become an acceptable and important category in psychiatry and related disciplines.[14] But with due respect to Erikson and others, it is precisely the profundity of the idea that makes its definition and implications still not only unclear but also mostly unexplored in detailed fashion.

Erikson understands trust correctly in paradoxical fashion. Trust without discrimination concerning untrustworthiness would be gullibility or sheer dependency. Yet trust must be real, for mistrust that over-generalizes from concrete instances of untrustworthiness can feed on itself and destroy all trust capacity. Whether one is dealing with the early years of a child's life, in which the foundation for basic trust is initiated in some degree or the child can survive only in stunted fashion, or with the exercise of discriminating trust in all subsequent periods of living, a conception of trust that does not attempt to articulate the paradoxical situation is intellectually useless and practically subversive.

Especially through the studies of René Spitz, Anna Freud, and others on babies deprived in affectional ways even though physical needs have been met, it has become a truism that trust cannot appear as a characteristic of young children if the care-taking persons are not trustworthy, and that this trustworthiness involves equally an affectional and relational quality along with meeting the physical needs.[15] To know and appreciate the strength of this need for trustworthiness in earliest childhood is a very important beginning for a deeper understanding of trust. But it is only a beginning.

Still thinking of the very small child, if his care-takers are considerably lacking in trustworthiness, he will manage to cope in some fashion, but with the probability that the defensive coping behavior, even though it may save his life, may continue as a permanent characteristic or readiness. Under such conditions the child will develop various kinds and degrees of suspiciousness, of withdrawal, or of subtle aggressiveness, which are not bad in a simple sense since they do produce a partially successful defense against the threat that he faces at that time. But they will be self-defeating over a longer period of time. Karl Menninger's theory of mental illness is based upon observation of and reflection about this kind of phenomenon.[16] Untrustworthy guides produce, therefore, an excess of suspicion over trust, and from then on the readiness of the person to trust what is trustworthy is impaired.

If we assume, on the other hand, situations in which the parents or care-takers are, at least relatively, trustworthy, how does trust emerge in the child? [17] Of course common sense tells us that it emerges from care, love, concern, proper diet, cuddling, and generally meeting the needs of the young child. But even the child of the most loving and competent parents has to be warned against taking candy or rides from strangers, walking into a fire, or falling out of windows. Today it is the custom to note that external disciplines of this kind do not harm the child if they are set within a relationship of basic trust justified by trustworthiness. I am sure that this is true in a general sense. But any misguided conclusion that there is a simple one-to-one relationship between parental trustworthiness and the emergence of trust-readiness in the child is contradicted daily by actual clinical experience. It is the job of parents both to love and to protect their children by measures of discipline before they are equipped to protect themselves.[18] But there is no formula for determining when the children are responding as the parents intend or otherwise. We know enough to detect gross distortions, but not much more.

Theoretically speaking, it may be unwise to speak of the quality we regard as desirable as simply "trust," or even "trust-readiness." For such a capacity in the subject person is not positive if it becomes attached to object people who are not trustworthy. Thus, effective statements about capacity for trust need to have their context articulated and not merely assumed. But there is no good substitute for the word "trust" to implement this intention.

We do well, however, to recognize the formidable nature of the problem of conceiving what real trust is and is not. How do we think about the child who must deal with persons who are low in trustworthiness, and who must therefore resort to some obvious devices for coping, but who nevertheless manages to generalize very little from these experiences, and who, when he encounters more trustworthy people, manages to trust them? This situation is very frequent among children of minority groups and the underprivileged. But we know very little about why so many children move beyond the chains of their environment.

All competent therapeutic work with children must deal with the questions of trust-readiness and trustworthiness of the human environment. The better the therapists are, however, the more skeptical they will be that they know in advance precisely what it means for them to be honestly trustworthy in relation to those they are trying to help. Recently I sat in on a group meeting with nine or ten young teen-aged hospitalized girls and their psychiatrist.[19] This was an open meeting where the girls could talk about nearly anything they wanted so long as it was reasonably decent. They discussed their privileges and restrictions, and also recent events that had happened to this member or that. Was Mary using her privileges appropriately? She had made one mistake with them; so what should happen now? Should the psychiatrist decree: no more mistakes, or we will crack down? Or should he, to be trustworthy, express his belief that Mary was moving generally in a constructive direction? What struck me most forcibly in this meeting was that the able psychiatrist was constantly, at least in his own mind and sometimes articulately with the girls, questioning himself about what it meant for him to be honestly trustworthy—both in his own eyes and theirs. Both perspectives were clearly important.

The extremes of cracking down or just being a good fellow were manifestly out. But excluding them was not enough. I found myself identifying very much with the psychiatrist's view that it requires daily re-assessment, not only of the others, but also of oneself in order to find the closest approximation to trustworthiness that is possible. What impressed me most was the psychiatrist's readiness to consider trustworthiness not merely as a matter of his own intent, but as equally involved with the message that got through to the girls. Thus, he had a built-in process of inquiry not only about them but also about himself.

If my description makes the psychiatrist sound unsure or vacillating, then I have not conveyed the real situation. By all ordinary standards, he was a strong person who knew where he stood. But he took extraordinary pains to investigate, after every encounter and even while it was going on, the question of what it meant for him to be genuinely trustworthy both to these girls as a group and to each girl individually. To do what he did required a constant and sometimes painful tension between his basic convictions about being trustworthy (which of course he would not change) and what this conviction meant in relational terms with the girls he was trying to help. His principles were essential but not enough. His way of bringing his convictions into relationship with the girls was always open to novelty, and indeed, his reflection upon the encounters might well alter some aspects of the way he considered and systematized his basic principles. If parents could take a similar kind of approach, I believe we would all be better off.

While I was at the University of Chicago, one of my students served as part-time chaplain at a school or institution for children who were severely handicapped physically. The project my student planned to carry out systematically was never completed, but he got far enough along with it to make me believe it is still a good idea. Many of the children were booked to die early, and most of them knew it. The children themselves demonstrated many degrees of adaptation to their handicaps and to their probable life span.

The first point that struck my student was that there was no obvious correlation between handicap and probably early death on the one side, and a generally positive or negative attitude about trust on the other side. He began to try to untangle the factors, not only the obvious ones such as what kind of home the child came from, but also the less obvious ones like the child's real feeling about a God if any. Unfortunately, my student was not able to complete his study. But I think it is precisely studies of this kind that are needed to advance our knowledge in this field.

Grim experiments about trust were conducted unwittingly in the Nazi concentration camps.[20] Three general conclusions became evident relating to trust. First, character in the ordinary sense, and ego-strength, were of help up to a point. To a degree, they could support. Second, many kinds of coping devices directed in a nonobvious manner at the untrustworthy people also helped. For instance, one physician I know became obsequious in behavior while retaining privately his conviction that everything about his keepers had to be distrusted. Third, in many instances the persons who were able longest to resist and to hold together were members of a small pledged group that hung together at all costs and, if necessary, let the welfare of others go.

One can hardly conceive a more extreme way in which to show the relation of discriminating mistrust to discriminating trust. Thank God that most of life is not concentration camps. There seem to be two guidelines about trust that emerge from study of those awful experiences. One is that trust should always be, in some proportion, corollary with the trustworthiness (or its absence) of others. Hence it is impossible to have trust without having also discriminating mistrust of the untrustworthy. The other is that trust, while it may be had alone up to a point, tends to be brittle without adequate group support.

Many of the psychic defense mechanisms or devices that psychoanalysis was the first to understand may be seen from the point of view of the trust question. Especially interesting is the automatic dynamism known as "identification with the aggressor," in which a person who is actually trying to subvert the interests of the subject is nevertheless the one who becomes the subject's object of identification.[21] So far as self-fulfillment goes, this device is a kind of reversion to unconscious devil-worship, and has no relationship to the Christian injunction to love our enemies. For loving our enemies, when we are able to do it, is neither imitating them nor denying in what respects they differ from us. What horrible psychic compulsion must be at work when the person who most threatens our interests becomes the model for imitation. That is the devil's providence.

In the light of the previous discussion, we do see some guidelines emerging about trust, its development, and its recovery after it has been partially lost. When trust is too undiscriminating, it moves into gullibility and dependency. When mistrust generalizes too far, it becomes anything from rudeness to paranoia. Trust may exist in such brittle fashion that one instance of untrustworthiness overturns it.

Trust as thin or brittle seems widespread in our day. For example, there is a considerable degree of concern among our people to try to put right some of the fundamental wrongs that have been done to deprived persons. But in far too many,

69

the concern dwindles or disappears in the face of a single act that makes the deprived people appear untrustworthy. Having been disadvantaged for a long time, it is inevitable that some of their actions to redress the balance will appear on the untrustworthy side. Disillusionment comes too easily to many persons as they examine such situations. Social betterment requires a longer view in which trust is not overturned by finding a few of its hopes not fulfilled immediately.

Since I believe that our insights into both trust and providence are important, both for religious people and for other men of goodwill, I have meditated on some possible way of stating them that would not have the language of traditional theology and yet would point beyond itself to the dynamic factors which that language has tried to capture. The reader may take the following few paragraphs as such an attempt. If I am capable of it, what would I like to be able to believe, and to act upon, about trust?

1. *As a realist I know that the world is a rough place, and I shall not be shattered or disillusioned when I find untrustworthiness just where I have least expected it. But the world is also full of potentialities, and I shall not permit my awareness of untrustworthiness to shield my perception away from serious pursuit of those potentials.*

2. *If I got everything I wanted at any moment of my life, that situation might well land me in worse difficulty than I am in now. I do not distrust all my wants. But I must be constantly self-critical about them. My wants as such are neither to be trusted nor distrusted automatically. I must sort them out to see what among them is to be trusted and pursued.*

3. *Even though most of life declares its ambiguity in capital letters, I know nevertheless that I have experienced great moments when the unambiguous, the wholly trustworthy, has been a part of my experience. I resolve not to become so suspicious that I shall fail to recognize such gifts, no matter where they may come from. On the other side, I pledge that I shall not concentrate so hard on grail hunting that I shall distort the ambiguities that make up most of my experience.*

4. *I have no apology for a prudent suspicion that tests out*

whatever or whoever claims to be trustworthy. But I shall permit this attitude to occupy only a preliminary place in my relationships. With persons I like, such an attitude soon disappears. But even with those I do not like or cannot understand, I shall endeavor to remain open to anything in the other that is worthy of trust.

5. If I can maintain this attitude of paradox, yet with a slant always in the direction of readiness to trust wherever there are partially trustworthy elements, then I shall feel that I am responding to something in the creation itself but in no way being forced or compelled.

For the person who is theologically oriented, it seems simple to move from such a secular statement to a declaration of attitude involving response to God's providential guidance. I pose the statement in secular language, however, partly to warn theologians against reverting to some past misinterpretations of providence, and partly to show those who may not share the theologian's perspective that there is something we are about that also concerns them.[22]

In suggesting several times how much we do not know about the dynamics of trust, I am not denigrating the knowledge we do have. But both in terms of research that will increase our knowledge and using effectively what we already know, we need always to put trust in a context that relates articulately to trustworthiness. When that is done, then even the most secular understandings of trust will deal in some fashion with the issues and experiences that have given rise to the doctrine of God's providence.

Providence in Calvinism

At the beginning of the chapter I argued that some of the ways in which God's providence had been dealt with in the sixteenth and especially the seventeenth centuries, above all by Calvinists, had included such extreme views that, in reaction to them, the teaching itself had tended to disappear. I suggested that the doctrine of double predestination, according to which God foreordains men to heaven or to hell, had a sound motive in its attempt to preserve God's rulership or sovereignty, but that the logical extreme of such teaching could not be consistent with the action of a God who loves mankind and has given him considerable freedom.[23] The present section will consider this matter further.

Before Calvinism became bogged down with double predestination, it developed three basic insights about God's providence. Although the third of these is the most ambiguous, I believe that even it, properly interpreted, can still have positive meaning. But of course I do not believe that our modern treatment of the doctrine can be confined to these points.

The first Calvinistic point was that providence is for our "preservation." If we wake up in the morning, we ought not to view this fact as a merely expected occurrence. Instead, we should reflect that, if God's providential care were not at work, the whole world might have burst in outer space during the preceding night. From a psychological point of view, providence as preservation calls for a certain kind of reflective attitude, not taking continuity for granted but recognizing that God's benevolence is exercised throughout creation at every moment. The attitude of response is to be gratitude. The enemy of such an attitude is simply taking whatever you have that you like for granted. The Calvinistic insight is that you short-change yourself by taking your preservation for granted.

The second category of providence in Calvinism was called "government," which was then a more general term than it is now. The substitution of "guidance" would make the basic idea closer to the modern vocabulary. In addition to preserving us, God is ready to supply those fundamental aspects of our needs that we cannot furnish for ourselves. Selectivity is of course involved. God will not supply to us just anything we happen to want, nor will he furnish what we can manage for ourselves. If we are attentive to his government or guidance, however, then we can apply the self-critical principle, and be alert to God's guidance at the same time we increase our own efforts to do what we can for ourselves.

The third dimension of providence was called "concurrence," and this is the most ambiguous of the three insights.

What the concurrence interpretation aimed at was this: If we really understand and agree that the purposes of God are good and holy, then we will "concur" with them even when, on other grounds, we might be against them.[24] The problem was, in practice, that concurrence implied simple obedience, of which the extreme result came when some people said they would be willing to be damned for the glory of God.

The positive side of concurrence teaching is well illustrated by the person who has problems, and who enters upon therapeutic work with some faith that his therapists can guide him constructively in a way that he cannot guide himself. If the therapists are competent both technically and as human beings, that faith should be justified. But as actual therapy experiences show, the sufferer may use his conviction, consciously or otherwise, to get the therapist to assume responsibility that is properly his own. Or his faith may become an appeasement strategy, apparently cringing in the face of authority but actually trying to keep the self from being touched by the need for change.

Belief in concurrence with God's will, therefore, frequently meant a limiting of the areas in which change would be tolerated. The person who declared that he was willing, if God so decreed, to be damned for the glory of God, might at the same time resist any change in outlook that would make him less cantankerous to his neighbors. The intent of concurrence was sound: a God who is for us and our development has better ideas about where we can move fruitfully than we have on our own.[25] But concurring with God, as if we knew precisely what he wants us to do, constitutes not only a kind of intellectual arrogance but also, in dynamic terms, the probability of ruling out in advance just those changes that would be most efficacious in our situation.

So far as they go, and especially with a critical eye on concurrence, these dimensions of providence as set forth in Calvinism still have relevance today. Yet they are also insufficient to deal with the paradox of what man can do for himself as against what he can do only with guidance from God.

Providence as preservation may turn into a genuflective ritual, as if God required us to acknowledge every hour on the hour that we would not be here without him. The narcissism of such a God would be intolerable to Christian insight. Providence as "government" or guidance may easily become a kind of acknowledgment of power, in which we admit that "almighty God" has his own holy agenda with which we must necessarily go along, but with the probable loss of the notion that what God most wants is for us to exercise our freedom responsibly. Providence as concurrence can very easily be turned into "identification with the aggressor" if one believes secretly that God is against us but has enough power so that we had better try to get on his side.

I believe that we shall have to find better categories than those of the old Calvinists in order to interpret the meaning of God's providence in our own day. Such categories, if we can find them, will be more rather than less paradoxical than those of the Calvinists. As we saw in the story of Lot, the angels accepted Lot's decision in favor of Zoar rather than the hills, but Mrs. Lot, refusing to think of any new direction at all, was doomed. Providence as preservation is basically a question of thanks and gratitude. Providence as "government" or guidance is open to empirical study about what we can and can not do for ourselves about the things that matter most. Providence as concurrence leads to the analysis of attitudes at different levels or dimensions of psychic life. The old ideas are, therefore, still potentially important. But they have to be seen and analyzed in a new way.

As we have discussed the three main Calvinistic points about providence, we begin to see dimly that, focused though they are on something recognizable as God's providential care of mankind, they could easily be made to leave the personal level of relationship between God and mankind and be put on an impersonal or cosmological level. That is what happened with predestination doctrine.[26] The attribute of God that is most important for the teaching about providence is his trustworthiness. To be trustworthy, however, and immensely significant to mankind, it must also be assumed that he has power. When the focus of attention became God's power rather than his benevolent trustworthiness, then the predestination teaching became possible, including the later double predestination, foreordination to salvation or damnation.

By the time the question became: Will the person go to heaven or to hell? it had been taken out of the realm that we know and shifted to speculation about what God intended in a future world of which we have no knowledge. The great disagreements were about precisely the realm of which we are ignorant. Whether we today are sympathetic toward the Calvinists and predestination, to the Armininans who questioned it, or to other groups of the past who took some position in between, what is now apparent is that the futurizing of man's situation, in a heaven or hell manner, was mistaken in shifting attention from what is going on here and now. Modern theologies need to understand the issues involved in controversies of the past. But they cannot solve their problems by opting for this or that position taken in the past. To be in the Calvinistic tradition today, it is not necessary or relevant to make much out of predestination. By the same token, to be in the Arminian or the Methodist tradition today does not require rejection of the Calvinistic insights into providence. What is needed for both groups is an updating of the old two-story universe in which the theological controversies were mainly about a future mode of existence of which we have no knowledge, and about which the biblical account is properly uninformative.

I am against predestination doctrine not so much for what it asserts (the sovereignty of God) as because it speaks to the wrong question: moving away from analysis of this world to speculative hope in another world unknown. But by the same token, I am equally against those in our theological history who argued that God did not predestine, but simply left decisions up to people. The position of the Calvinists was precise but aimed at a world we know nothing about. Their opponents were less logical but equally concerned with some other world. In my judgment, they both dealt with the wrong question. Perhaps not wrong in their day, but wrong in ours.

Before closing out our discussion of predestination, we

should note that there are several modern secular versions of this teaching, even worse than the original because they have not the saving grace of a religious question. Middle-class parents today assume that their children will, at the very least, do as well as they have done. But then comes one child who does not conform to expectations. All along, without knowing it, the family has had a predestinarian kind of expectation. It may have paid off with some of the children. But when the nonconformist appears, they are completely baffled. They were so sure—and now look what they have. The more open family, less sure of itself and engaged in more self-criticism, has a better time when the tough problems appear. It is the assured family with an unacknowledged predestinarian trend that has the worst time coming to terms with the actual situation.

Our society has a very moralistic form of predestination in judging what makes children turn out this way or that. If a teen-ager becomes sexually promiscuous, or smokes marihuana, or steals cars, or goes hippie, then the culture generally assumes that the parents are at fault. It is assumed that the parents provided all the "pre" that has become involved in the "destination." [27]

At least for those persons whose own children are not in such a situation, this neat separation of white hats from black hats may be comforting. But even the most rudimentary reflection shows that judgments of this kind are not to be trusted. We really know very little about why this teen-ager does this and another does something else. The parents whose children, whatever the reason, are doing rather well are very much like the old predestinationists who assumed they were on God's side. Their evaluation of the children on the other side may, therefore, be devoid of both human sympathy and of a knowledge of the complexity of all human personality.

Unacknowledged secular conceptions of predestination all conspire to get the subjects off the hook, whether the people in question (mainly children) are doing what the parents want or not. If Johnny is doing fine by parental judgments, then parents take all the credit. If Johnny is in trouble, then the cause is his college, or the culture, or teen-age mores, or anything but the relation of Johnny to his parents. The point is that there is a great deal of misguided predestination doctrine in existence today going under quite other terms. And as usual, the behavioral response is to try to get the self off the hook.

In the movement of sound providence doctrine to dubious predestination teaching I have made brief allusion to the matter of power. But this factor remains to be analyzed dynamically. I agree with my ancestors that God could not be genuinely trustworthy unless he had some power to back up his convictions and actions. God has decided, however, not to be omnipotent. If he were omnipotent, there would be no freedom in his creatures and especially in man. But his decision not to be all-powerful does not mean that he has ducked power altogether, whether in himself or in his creatures.

My Reformation ancestors became rather too much aware of God's power and did not sufficiently recognize that, with God's steadfastness, his power meant trustworthiness. Even today we have people who will recognize the power of God only if something happens that known laws apparently cannot encompass. Such views represent an "accidental" or "accretive" or even esoteric conception of the power of God. It is not that I am against recognizing the hand of God in unusual circumstances. But I refuse to permit the concept of God's power to be judged by such situations. God is around all the time, whether we recognize him at work or not.

Part of the argument for the teaching about providence related legitimately to God's power as well as to his benevolence; namely, whatever powers there are dealing with the ambiguities of human life, the basic power is a benevolent God, not chance fate or enmity or divided minds. When we re-examine predestination doctrine of the seventeenth century in the light of this position, it acquires more relevance.[28] The underlying intent of the teaching was to declare the positive meaningfulness of whatever in the universe responds to the aspirations of man, and to deny that that other something is negative, vengeful, ambiguous, or of two minds. Looking at predestination teaching from that perspective, it makes a lot more sense. Directed against fate and meaninglessness, the notion of God's having an idea in mind in advance was a guarantee that man's world is meaningful. To make that possible, God had to have some power.

The trouble appeared when the necessary notion of God's power, allied to his being for man and in no way against his development, was cosmologized into double predestination doctrine, and equally when, in Wesley and Arminius, such allegations were denied. What must be got rid of is not power in itself, for how could a God be importantly benevolent without some kind of power, but the notion that power in God's hands could possibly be separated from benevolence and love. My suspicion is that Arminius and Wesley were closer to the right answer than were the Calvinists of their time. But they all gave answers to a somewhat distorted question.

I am personally and professionally a grateful but not uncritical inheritor of the Calvinistic tradition. Since it was mainly my ancestors who turned a generally sound doctrine of God's providence into a predestinarian teaching that became so inhuman as to invite both flat disagreement and also evasion, I feel a special responsibility to rescue the core teaching from the accretions. The core question is not about what God decides in advance concerning babies going to heaven or hell. It is, instead, about our understanding of God's readiness to help us precisely where we are unable to help ourselves. God's handiwork is evident only when we really need it, and only about the questions that we would decide wrongly without it. Any man or group must decide for itself whether there is or is not such a factor in actual experience. But if there is, then its name is God's providence. It will not provide our food, pay our mortgage or taxes, or read our books for us. Those things we can do for ourselves. But when we know not where to turn, or are deficient in just precisely what we need by way of supplies, that is exactly where God, in his providence, will provide special equipment.

The Relevance of Providence

Today we are in grave need of a doctrine of providence not only in relation to our personal lives, or our lives within the church, but also in terms of relating to and aiding our society to achieve humane aims. It is precisely because our society does not have a properly paradoxical view of providence that our culture fluctuates between the greatness of our potentialities and the horror of our gigantic social problems. The space program has become the cardinal symbol of our potentialities (and its budget has been cut), and the ghetto areas have become the principal symbol of our problems (their budget has also been cut). "Business as usual" in our society is inclined to be almost equally suspicious of problems and potentialities. In budget terms, each is likely to be cut when the going gets rough.

Our dimes say, "In God we trust." For an energetic people who have shown so much energy on getting ahead, this is a strange national motto unless it assumes some factors that the coins cannot specify. Coins may of course represent shortcuts in their mottoes. But the fact is that we have no right to look to God for what we can do for ourselves. Hence, there is a proper paradox between trusting in God and working like the devil. There need be no contradiction.

I suppose my final argument is that, whether we are dealing with religious or secular man, we need a conviction that is like the providence doctrine of old. Secular man knows that he needs to be sensitive to and analytical about trust, that he must be suspicious at some times and yet not let suspicion-readiness overpower him, and that discovery of the bases of trust in the other, however qualified, is the *sine qua non* for getting on with all kinds of programs personal, communal, or even international. My argument has been that he must consider not only his own discriminating capacity for trust in all his decisions, but also his best evaluation (even if it has holes in it) of the trustworthiness of the other in making his decisions about trusting. I have also argued that this general process of decision-making is very similar to what the teaching about providence is about. The general doctrine is no substitute for the analysis in specific situations, but the analysis of specific situations is likely to be restricted if not done in the larger context.

Our world, as Paul Tillich rightly noted, is full of boundary situations.[29] This fact is easy enough to see among countries, races, classes, and value systems, to say nothing of the more subtle dimensions of Presbyterian and Methodist, lower middle class and upper middle class, southern background as against northern, and much else. Even the most competent husband and wife live in more of a boundary situation than they may realize until conflicts make them get help and realize what has happened. Complete and infallible trust is impossible at a human level. But so, happily, is complete untrustworthiness. The degree of the positive qualities that we can summon by whatever means, whether in personal or in larger social matters, may be determinative of the future both of ourselves and of our world. We do well to think of God's providence as just possibly tipping the scales in the right direction. But that could happen only if we had done everything in our own power. God is providential, but he is neither a big daddy nor a supporter of irresponsible contracts.

Chapter 4
SIN AND SICKNESS

Even if the average man is in church, he will attempt to escape if he is asked about theology. When pressed, he will be vague about grace, providence, the atonement, and many other concepts in the theological vocabulary. But if he is asked about sin, he may be sure that he knows what it is. And he will very probably be wrong. There is no theological idea that has fallen victim to such widespread misunderstanding.

Our discussion will first examine the basic meaning of sin in the Western theological tradition, then consider the principal metaphors that have been used to convey this meaning, and further the forms and the dynamics of sin. Finally the discussion will focus on sickness, its nature and dynamics, and we shall conclude by suggesting the sense in which sickness and sin are and are not inherently related.

The Meaning of Sin

In both Judaism and Christianity, the meaning of sin cannot be grasped without keeping two presuppositions firmly in mind. The first is that God is for us, is unambiguously for our fulfillment, and is not of two minds about the world he has created. The second is that God has given his creatures considerable freedom, limited of course, but real within its limits. It follows from these two presuppositions that God values freedom in his creatures so much that, despite his desire for their fulfillment, he is unready to bring about this consummation from outside without their cooperation and initiative. If we do not see sin in this kind of context, we misunderstand it altogether in the tradition.

If God were of two minds about us, then we could never

know when we were misusing our freedom. Getting in trouble would not mean sin but bad luck, catching God on the wrong day. If, on the other hand, our freedom were entirely an illusion, then there could be no possible human factors involved when things go wrong, and it would follow that God himself is accountable for the difficulty. Therefore, the context of God's benevolence and man's freedom is essential for understanding the meaning of sin.

When men misuse their freedom, so that there is movement away from human fulfillment, then sin is being committed. The sin is against what has been traditionally called the will of God. But since that will is for man's fulfillment consistent with respect for his freedom, then sin is also against the self and other people in a corollary way. In the biblical perspective, sin is not just a matter of morals especially in the modern sense. It is a basic decision against the God who wants the proper fulfillment of man.[1]

In the realism of the Old Testament account, the recognition is clear that sinners may get what they want at least for a time, that the wicked may indeed flourish while the righteous man has a rough time. But in that event the wicked man, in not acknowledging his sin as sin, or repenting of it, puts himself in a corner. He may flourish for a time, but the biblical account suggests that his temporary flourishing is not only against the general fulfillment of the people but is also against his own fulfillment properly understood.[2]

It was implicit from the start, but made articulate only later, that sin is never unaccompanied by God's gracious effort, consistent with respect for man's freedom, to aid the sinner, person or nation, to repent and alter course. If that effort succeeded, then there was the "conviction" of sin. The person who is convicted of sin by his own standards, realizing that he has injured his own fulfillment as well as that of his fellowman, then appropriately recognizes that God's grace was at work upon and within him even before he repented. Thus, we cannot properly think of sin outside this whole process or course of events.[3] What separates sin from mere evil-doing is the context of God's grace and providence in which it is understood.

In insisting on this context, theology is setting forth an intuition about the relationship of needs and wants as discussed in the previous chapter. Even the wicked man catering only to his own wants, according to this view, is nevertheless trying at some deeper level of being to meet his legitimate needs. Perhaps his ways of acting are deeply injurious to him and to other people. But God is attentive to the potential repentance as well as to the harmful acts. Thus sin can never be mere blaming or name-calling.

Whether we are dealing with persons or institutions, there is a rough analogy between awareness of sin as diagnosis, concerned about what is wrong, and repentance of sin as either therapy or constructive change, concerned about righting whatever is wrong. One reason today why we have extended the notion of illness over the concepts of former times is precisely to prevent the wrong or misguided action from being separated from the potential processes of therapy or change.[4] A wicked man may also be a sinner, but the redeeming core in the concept of sin is of no meaning to him until he is helped to repent of it. The reason we have the concept of sin is not, therefore, because people are wicked, but rather because, even though men do evil things that defeat themselves and others, there are means available for change in a constructive direction. If this were not so, then we could simply dispense with sin, and talk only about evil, wickedness, crime, and destruction.

Also implicit from the beginning, but made articulate only later, was the idea of "original sin" as well as "actual sin."[5] To assert that sin has an "original" or given dimension means that, over and above whatever freedom the person had that he misused, there are social and historical forces at work within the man and within society that require repentance and constructive change. It was as clear to the ancients as it is to us today that many of man's acts are conditioned by social and historical forces in the face of which he is partially bound. This fact is acknowledged by understanding sin to have an "original" aspect or dimension. Such a conviction helps to prevent the idea of sin from degenerating into blame, especially blame of the individual person. There is also another consequence, that if society as well as persons need to repent of sinful ways, then the potential for proper social action is not absent. God is much more interested in getting society to repent, recognize its errors, and get on the right track than he is in punishing it.

What is the relation between sin and guilt? From the theological point of view, the meaning of guilt in relation to sin is redemptive, that is, the acknowledgment of guilt is equivalent to repentance over sin.[6] Thus, the proper sensing of real guilt means that the sin is being both recognized and repented of, and thus that there is acceptance of the work of God's grace in making needed changes.

In Christian history guilt also came to be understood in a forensic or penal sense, and the detailed canon laws that emerged frequently obscured the underlying dynamics that were concerned with effecting constructive change whenever possible, so that a persistent sinner was cut off only as a very last resort.[7] Although law is necessary in both church and society, and performs many constructive functions including protection of the person from arbitrary decisions of social institutions, law that hardens into legalism misses the understanding of guilt that is primary in theology and is always inherently related to the potentialities for repentance and constructive change.

Modern psychiatry and related disciplines demonstrated convincingly that a great many painful and nagging feelings of guilt are misplaced, i.e., not justified by rational considerations, or detached from the relationships out of which they grew and then attached to less threatening objects or even trivialities.[8] The church should not have been surprised that guilt feelings often conceal more than they reveal. Long ago the Roman Catholic Church recognized that "scrupulous" persons are unable to accept assurances of forgiveness as the normal person can when he repents, confesses, and resolves to do better. Today we see such scrupulosity as a form of obsessionalism. The person is driven by the dynamic forces operating within him, so that his feelings of guilt no longer have their intended meaning, namely, helping him to constructive change through repenting.

In recent years the psychiatric disciplines have had increasing acquaintance with persons who seem devoid of guilt feelings even when they have plainly injured other people as well as themselves. The dynamics of such persons are still a partially moot question. Did they fail, in the process of development, to acquire any real capacity for empathy with the feelings of others? Or did they come to hide their capacity because, when they exercised it, they found themselves to be exploited? Are they weak in the area of conscience, or do they have consciences which were turned underground by events?

Both society and theology become concerned when, whatever the dynamics, there seems to be no evidence of guilt feelings even when harm has been done. But they should also be bothered when guilt feelings hang on and on. The function of guilt feelings is to produce repentance, which is a readiness to change, and then to proceed with the change, after which the guilt feelings should cease to be persistent. These remarks apply especially to guilt and guilt feelings about personal actions or inactions.[9]

A somewhat different perspective about guilt feelings is needed in relation to situations and conditions that go beyond the self and its immediate environment. There is no chance of basic remedies for the poverty and degradation of the city slums or in the other side of the world unless we have a lively sense of concern, and hence some continuing and activating sense of guilt, in relation to those conditions. This is why Reinhold Niebuhr believed, rightly, that the conscience of the Christian should always be uneasy.[10] The unease should not be to paralyze action but to stimulate it constructively, no matter how ambiguous the situation, in the best directions we can now conceive. A program for "eliminating" the sense of guilt would be monstrous. But people cannot have a chance of developing appropriate concern for society's underprivileged populations until they have been helped to get rid of the burden of personal guilt.

In this preliminary survey of the basic meaning of sin, we may ask to what extent sin takes place, as the prayer book of the Episcopal Church puts it, "in thought, word, or deed."

"Deed" is clear-cut, while "thought" and "word" are not. Furthermore, our ancestors omitted reference to "feeling." Thomas Aquinas declared that sin was always *actus*, a Latin word that has a broader meaning than "act" does in English.[11] Thomas knew that what today we would call an obsessional or compulsive desire or preoccupation could make the subsequent act inevitable. Therefore, *actus* was held to include this kind of preoccupation. Thomas' decision was, however, far from equating a passing thought or word or desire with the deed. The critical question is whether thought, word, or feeling become enmeshed in a dynamic pattern that compels action of a certain kind, or whether they can still be dealt with as they ought to be, as ingredients of the dynamic mixture that have to be appraised and decided upon. Unless they have reached the point of compulsion or obsession, thought, word, and feeling are still open to inspection.

When we reflect, in relation to larger social concerns, on the many subtle ways in which our acts deprive other people in economic, racial, or political ways, it is clear that we need to repent of these actions even though we have not, as individuals, decided on them.

The fundamental meaning of sin, then, in Western theology is not supplying a special term for either dire or naughty deeds. It is an attempt to link the means of change and reparation with the nature of the trouble. As theology has said on many occasions, the news of sin is good news. For the man or group that recognizes its sinfulness is repenting and moving toward needed change. This recognition is very different from merely seeing that evil has been done.

Metaphors About Sin

Several metaphors, representing analogies about types of relationships, have been used to try to convey the meaning of sin. The effectiveness of each has tended to vary with the patterns of different ages. This discussion will emphasize the *three principal metaphors* that have been used from biblical days until the present.

The first, and very long-lasting, metaphor has seen sin as *rebellion*.[12] If we think of an ancient larger Jewish household, whether in its nomadic days or upon settling down on the farm, it is plain that the whole organization had to be tightly run or the social order would have broken down. Residual authority was vested in the senior paternal figure, later supplemented on the area and district level by judges and then kings. Whatever disturbed the order and activity of the household was understood as rebellion against the authority of the head. For anyone not to do his job was itself a mark of rebellion. One of King David's sons seduced his half-sister and left her a nervous wreck.[13] Another drove the first son away from home because of his deed. Still another founded an opposition party and nearly succeeded in ousting his father.[14] In such a culture, it was easy to see rebellion as the key clue to sin.

In a more sophisticated form, however, sin has continued to be interpreted as rebellion through many ages. For a long time the patterns were external because the patterns of political authority were also external.[15] Yet as early as Augustine in the fourth century it was seen that "hybris," or pride as we usually translate from the Greek, is dynamically not so much specific acts against a proper authority figure as it is the push to exceed our proper human limits. In the most searching modern analysis of sin, Reinhold Niebuhr brought "hybris" back as the key to much sin.[16]

Sin as rebellion or pride carries the connotation of aggressiveness. There may or may not be open defiance, because ignoring or evading authority may be more aggressively successful than frontal attack. And those who are on the other side, who are the authority figures and who have what they want, defend it by naked aggression only as a last resort. In short, we must look beyond the obvious to find hybris as it actually operates in today's world.

The insights of psychiatry and related disciplines into the nature and dynamics of aggression are of increasing value.[17] We know that this capacity is not in itself negative, that without it we might also lack creativity. We know that some over-aggressiveness conceals weakness and requires guidance and redirection. We have learned that the outwardly passive modes of aggression may be the most difficult to change or even to get at. Theology may need to find a new vocabulary in which to speak of the hybris that is like passive aggressiveness, or that which appears as a rocklike standing pat on one's own class, race, or nation.

Are the extreme rebellious movements of some teen-age and young adult groups today to be understood as hybris? Insofar as they use bombs and guns and other means of violence, that may be a justifiable conclusion. But that part of the middle-aged adult group which regards hair length and bare feet as no less wicked than bombs and guns, and justifies the use of the latter by its agents, is certainly no less guilty of hybris. Thus, if we analyze closely and are not thrown off the track by surface appearances, the metaphor of rebellion or hybris for understanding sin has in no way become irrelevant, even though its forms have changed since the agricultural days of the Old Testament.

The second principal metaphor about sin appeared in the New Testament as *missing the mark*.[18] The analogy was to throwing a spear. If you are in battle, it makes no difference whether you miss your enemy by an inch or a mile. Either way, your fate is likely to be the same.

This analogy of missing the mark was very meaningful in a day when both Jews and Greeks, of all ages and both sexes, were being urged to receive the treasure of the Christian gospel so that they might be released from whatever had bound them and in whatever degree. Many people were inclined to say, "I have sinned only a little." From the point of view of not having been heinously wicked, no doubt that was true. But if that fact were used as excuse against the need for the gospel, obviously the early Christians were against it. So they framed the message about sin in terms of missing the mark. Unless you receive the new life, no matter the degree of your previous wickedness, you will receive the equivalent of death.

Just as the rebellion metaphor could be misused to condemn any possible criticism of the status quo, so the analogy to missing the mark could be and was sometimes used in very legalistic and moralistic fashion. Minute details of conduct were alleged to be as important as things of genuine significance, and those who believed in making distinctions were given short shrift.[19]

Revivalists often used the metaphor of missing the mark to get people to walk down the sawdust trail, their converts usually being ordinary people with unresolved guilt feelings about small matters of personal conduct. They were seldom successful with unscrupulous landlords, robber barons, or smug exploiters.

Missing the mark is an analogy that may of course be used in sophisticated rather than crude fashion. One drink does not produce alcoholism, but reliance on one drink taken often enough can lead in that direction. A single injection of heroin does not produce drug addiction, but not many more injections are required to achieve that condition. A nation is not necessarily ruled by a militaristic spirit because it has standing armed forces and weapons for prudential protection of its people and territory. But it is not easy to draw a line between such protection and a massive effort at security that does produce a spirit of militarism.

There are many conditions in life in which a near miss, while not so bad as a mile's, tends to lead on to graver consequences. By the same token, the person or group that takes the apparently small thing seriously may be making more progress than it realizes. For example, if a person who is in psychiatric therapy has some strong compulsions and one week is able to report that he did not engage in the compulsive behavior—this is not a small thing but a harbinger of significant change. He may have thought about it, talked to himself about it, or pictured it in his mind. But if he did not do it, he is more than a small step ahead. On the larger social scale, something similar might well prove to be true about something like disarmament.

The third principal metaphor that has been used about sin is *isolation* or *alienation* or *estrangement*, or, generally speaking, being cut off. This analogy has seemed to have peculiar meaning in our own day, although its roots go further back into history. Yet the appeal of the metaphor is comparatively modern as against the other two that have been noted.

THEOLOGICAL DYNAMICS

In a medieval household, whatever its virtues of organic community life, personal concern for each by all, and guilds to foster both craftsmanship and self-respect, there was no privacy in the modern sense of the term.[20] Not even the nobility had private rooms in the sense that they could be sure that others would not enter. Very small children lived in "the room" with their parents. By the time they were seven or eight, they left home to work in houses of wealthier people, but never thought of having their own rooms. Even the houses of the wealthy had all kinds of people coming in and out of all the rooms.

With the possible exception of remote rural areas, such an environment could not even have conceived of alienation unless in terms of prison captivity. Isolation could become a dreadful idea only after architecture, industrialism, individualism, and the notion of privacy had increased to a considerable degree. That movement came only in preliminary form in the fourteenth and fifteenth centuries, moved a bit faster but still haltingly in the sixteenth and seventeenth centuries, and did not get into high gear until the eighteenth century or the first part of the nineteenth. Today we value privacy highly. But we also dread isolation. Especially if one is poor or disadvantaged, he may find himself today alone in a sense that neither king nor serf knew in the middle ages. Even suburbanites know that the line between a desired privacy and an enforced isolation may be very thin.

If estrangement were only something forced upon us by the conditions of our society, and we were in no way accomplices in our alienated condition, then this metaphor could not be about human sin. Instead, we could deal with isolation in the same way we try to handle disease microbes, as threats from the outside against which we devise specific remedies.

But alienation or estrangement is a metaphor for sin because, even though many of the conditions that produce it lie beyond us as persons, we always have some complicity in the resulting condition. The shy girl at the party may be pining for popularity; yet she may be most resistive to the kindest person present who tries to get her involved. There are dynamic reasons why she is not involved, and neither she nor her would-be helper can get over them quickly. If she gets the kind of assistance, or finds it out for herself, that enables her to make changes in the dynamics, then she may relax at the party and become less isolated and more related. If that happens, she can understand her previous condition as isolation, partly compelled but partly with her own compliance. Even very isolated people, such as those who have strong schizophrenic trends, under competent therapy become better at relating to others and eventually understand that they have had a hand in producing their condition. That hand may have been very small, but it is the part that therapy can work on.

In the last few years we have witnessed a widespread revulsion against pollution of many kinds. The pollution has been piling up for a long time, and a few far-sighted persons have been warning about it. It still remains to be seen whether effective or only token action will be taken. But what made possible the present outcry of indignation and repentance was the recognition that we have all had complicity in the situation. The pollution is rightly understood to be not only dirt and disease but also an estrangement of man from nature.

Paul Tillich used isolation and estrangement as his central concept of sin, and succeeded in conveying the idea to many people not holding traditional theological notions.[21] Tillich usually stressed the conditions of society that keep persons separated. That is the "original sin" dimension of estrangement. It is always present and often decisive. It becomes decisive most of the time, however, only when persons refuse to accept their partial complicity in the situation. This last is the "actual sin" dimension of isolation. Both aspects need to be kept in mind if the metaphor of isolation for sin is to be genuinely meaningful. If one simply blames the arrangements of society for the existing estrangement, he may be demonstrating what psychiatrists call unresolved narcissism instead of repenting for his part in the situation.

This discussion of the three leading metaphors to convey the meaning of sin has tried to show the dynamics involved in each conception, the basic meaning of each and how it may be distorted, and the continuing utility of each if brought up to date.

Finally, we may note briefly a few of the other metaphors that have been used to explicate sin. One of them is *disobedience*. This term came from words that originally meant "not hearing." As Kenneth R. Mitchell has rightly suggested, disobedience in the sense of not hearing is well demonstrated in what Catholics have called the "scrupulous" person, who simply does not hear when he is assured that his sin is forgiven.[22] Probably the word "disobedience" itself has permanently lost its original meaning. But in psychiatric therapy, psychological studies of perception, and modern explorations into communication, the dynamics of not hearing are yielding rich fruit. If not really hearing is one way to understand sin, then we are acquiring some new insights into how to help people to hear again.

Another metaphor for sin has been the general notion of *indulgence*, or what Reinhold Niebuhr called "sensuality." [23] By this he meant that the person lives beneath his limits, as the proud person lives above them. The person sinks back, whether into vices or indifference. From a dynamic point of view, he lacks the ego strength to affirm and pursue his goals. In Freudian terms, he does not have control of his Superego.

All these analogical attempts to describe sin are still useful, but they may require serious supplementation in the future if the basic idea is not to be lost.

Forms of Sin

No Western religious group has been without some kind of classification of sins. But there have been real differences in the degree to which classification has been stressed. Generally speaking, legalistic interpretations have paid more attention to the forms of sin, while groups taking the miss-the-mark point of view (an inch or a mile) have tended to regard all sin in any degree as equally worthy of serious attention.[24] The latter have tended, thus, to be perfectionists. As we now know, the dynamics of legalism and of perfectionism are very similar; so we need to take care that our own analysis does not fall into such traps.

Traditional Roman Catholic moral theology made a sharp distinction between so-called "mortal" or more serious sins, and "venial" or less serious sins.[25] The intent behind the distinction was to use appropriate degrees of persuasion or force as relevant to the heinousness of the sinful act. In practice only good people tended to confess venial sins. The rigidity of the older categories is now under wide attack in the Catholic Church, and the classification system of the future will certainly have more flexibility than did that of the past. In shaking off its rigidities about sin, however, I hope that Catholicism will not discard classification altogether. Even now we know that there are some types of disposition and action which, though they appear small, tend to lead on to dire consequences. On the other hand, there are many things which other people do which we do not like but which carry no clearly bad consequences either for themselves or for us. Scientific inquiry can help us reach a better classification scheme than was available in the past.

While traditional Catholicism assumed a legalistic position in classifying sins, traditional Protestantism tried to avoid such classification so far as it could. Its intent was in keeping with the miss-the-mark metaphor about sin, holding that any sin at all was equally hateful in God's eyes. Theoretically, this meant that a Protestant Christian was supposed to come humbly before God with his own sin and not think up reasons that would make the other man's sin appear worse than his own. In practice, this approach often meant that local customs developed their own classification system with insufficient criticism on theological grounds. New England had its scarlet letter for the unmarried mother. Even today, the Protestant distaste for any official classification of sins is shown in the use of the term "Christian ethics" as against the Catholic term "moral theology." [26] It seems time that Protestants realized that some degree of classification is inevitable, and that the question is whether it will be on sound grounds, flexible, and supported by hard data on how small beginnings do or do not lead to dire consequences.

The most famous popular Western classification of sins was in the seven deadly sins of the Middle Ages. When I did a modest study of them some years ago, I found that a standard list had been formulated only in the late Middle Ages, and that previous lists had varied a good deal.[27] I was pleased to discover that Thomas Aquinas had no such list, even though he listed virtues until they ran out of his inkwell. I suspect that Thomas realized that, if you appeared to have a neat assortment of really serious sins, anybody with enough brains could figure out how to keep his own propensities out of the list.

As the seven deadly sins took final shape, they were: pride or hybris, covetousness, lechery, anger, envy, gluttony, and accidie. At first glance, the surprising fact is that nothing in this list confines itself to isolated acts. Everything is characterological, related to tendencies of repetition. Acts are not absent, but they are implied to be inevitable consequences of tendencies of character.

We have already discussed hybris or pride as one way of seeing the root of sin. Here it is presented in a more modest way, as a form of sin, but still heading the list. Covetousness and envy are similar in that they want what others have, but they are different in that covetousness refers to possessions and envy to status or privilege. Gluttony and lechery are alike in that they mean taking too much of what, within limits, is all right. Anger in this list means not simply an interior reaction, as to injustice, but an uncriticized or impulsive expression in action, or a continuing chilly resentment.

The surprising entry in the list is accidie. There is no proper English translation of this word. The usual translation of "sloth" is misleading. In the Middle Ages this was the term applied, for instance, to a monk who went through a period of going stale on his prayers and other duties, going through the motions but with no zest, and sometimes being literally unable to carry out many of his duties. The modern term "anomie" gives some of the flavor of accidie, but it is far from precise as a synonym. The original term implied a form of sin, not simply a cut-off brought about by factors wholly beyond one's control. Something about the person himself was involved in a form of compliance.

The first six deadly sins are apparent in modern as in medieval life even if their details have changed. Do we also have accidie today, or was it something limited to monastic living? I am more and more inclined to the view that, if we shift just a little the way medieval Christians understood accidie, then we have some very important intuitions about a truly alarming form of sin in today's world.

Medieval Christians saw accidie in the monk who tried consciously very hard but felt empty within. The monk suffered because his conscious self wanted to feel committed and immersed and positive in his faith. Modern dynamic theory would, however, ask what forces beneath the surface were impeding the monk's ability to invest himself in that to which he was consciously committed. The specifics might differ from monk to monk. In one there might be strong and unacknowledged aggressiveness; in another, a tyrannical Superego; in another, an unresolved Oedipus complex; and in still others, many more psychic complexities. But in all instances the result would be seen as dynamic or compulsive indifference, zestlessness, or anomie. The fact that the monk suffered consciously from his condition would be regarded as a good sign, that he was still a candidate for getting over his condition. Such an analysis suggests that the medieval describers of accidie included in their description the first stage of therapy or getting out of the condition. In other words, the conscious suffering was not part of the illness but the first step in its cure.

Reinterpreted in this way, then, accidie becomes that kind of human response in which there is a partial psychic paralysis. It is partial or the person soon would be dead. It never appears stark and alone, for there are always automatic efforts to cope with it. The coping may take the form of living only in the immediate and forced environment (the family, for instance) and withdrawing all concern from anything beyond, even though the larger factors are also vital to one's fulfillment. The coping may also assume the form of anomie, in which no zest is felt about anything but one rationalizes that society has taken meaning from him. Or the attempt to cope may take dramatic forms as in the mental patients studied by Anton T. Boisen, who thought the world was coming to an immediate end and they had a special mission to perform.[28]

We still have a few of Boisen's kind of patients. We have some anomie people, some of whom disguise the abdication of personal responsibility under their criticism of the inhumanity of society. But above all we have the people who seem indifferent to every order of reality other than that which touches them immediately. Whether they feel happy about home base or not may be important practically, but it does not touch the basic dynamics. However they feel about self and mate and home, they are compulsively indifferent to anything beyond. Their basic zestlessness has been translated into myopic indifference to anything but that which is immediate, near, and obtrusive. They are under partial compulsion (but they also comply) to restrict severely that part of the world (all of which in fact affects them) to which they will give either attention or interest. In actual fact they may have little zest about even the obtrusive things and relationships, but their human instinct for coping may not permit them to realize that even when it is true. If their zest for the near relationships is authentic, then there is something to build on to other areas, i.e., such positive feelings would be the first steps in constructive change and not simply part of the problem—as with the medieval monk who suffered under his accidie.

On some nights I have had the dreadful vision that the accidie people of today are the "silent majority." If indifference, too, must be understood dynamically, and not merely in terms of laziness about positive action, then the situation could be alarming not so much because of the numbers (the "majority") as because the zestlessness of this group is enormously closer to despair than it realizes. Accidie in this form makes it impossible to take account of the ambiguities of our world and still emerge with a vote for and not against the world. Since complexity increases, accidie as defined here (rightly or wrongly) becomes as great an enemy of cultural advance as hybris. If we set out to destroy the world, the best combination we could find would be dictators convinced that they are right and accidie sinners who couldn't care less about anything beyond the immediate environs.

My fascination with the dynamics and implications of accidie, as a form of sin, may have diverted the reader from the intent of this section, which is to ask about how we should understand the forms of sin. What is crucial in all sin is that, despite an "original" or given dimension, there is always some degree of potential control of behavior and character; therefore, the conviction or awareness of sin is itself the mark of a step ahead. But this fact does not alter the need to ask whether a typology of sin can be devised that helps to foster the purposes of repentance of sin, and consequent release into new freedom.

Any such scheme that may be devised must take with seriousness the important distinction between behavior that is compelled and that which retains various degrees of freedom. Even in the most obsessional person freedom is never wholly extinguished. And even in the most "self-realizing" person there are elements of compulsion. With my general suspicion of mathematical models, it is difficult for me to admit what follows. But I must come reluctantly to the conclusion that it could be possible to appraise degrees of responsibility, and therefore of actual sinfulness, in specific persons and situations. I hope we shall never get the levels on a computer. But even a computer, subservient to human judgments, would be enormously better than the judgments we now have.

At this time I am certainly not up to devising a new scheme for the forms of sin that takes account of what is known about the dynamics of this or that form of intent, character, or behavior. But as against my own Protestant tradition which has regarded all such efforts as vain, I plead for a new look. No more than contemporary Catholics do I want a return to a legalistic lockstep system of assessing penalties in this or that degree. But I want a realistic assessment of which mild behaviors tend to lead to dire consequences, and which do not.

I can no longer tolerate the Protestant illusion that, since all sin is sinful, let us therefore have no typologies at all. With the aid of psychological and social science, we have new grounds on which—once we understand the basic meaning of sin as rebellion against or alienation from the God who wills our fulfillment—we can give some clues about what is more sinful than something else, and precisely why.

In closing out this discussion of the forms of sin, with its plea to take this matter seriously again with the help of the empirical disciplines, I want to preach a brief sermon with the help of the apostle Paul. In the latter part of his short letter to the Galatians, Paul defines the "works of the flesh" that impede the "fruits of the spirit." [29] Here is Paul's fifteen-item list of the works of the flesh: immorality, impurity, licentiousness, idolatry, sorcery, enmity, strife, jealousy, anger, selfishness, dissension, party spirit, envy, drunkenness, carousing. It is clear that the "flesh" (sarx in Greek, quite different from the Greek word for body, soma) is, in modern words, a matter of attitude and character rather than simply about isolated acts. The majority of Paul's terms refer to actions which, in moderation, are good, and become "works of the flesh" only in excess. But even those terms that condemn any behavior at all (such as sorcery) involve underlying attitude rather than isolated behavioral instances.

Paul's list is, I believe, less sophisticated than that of the deadly sins of the medieval world. Both lists remind us, however, that all competent Western theological insights about sin stress underlying attitude and character and not simply behavior as such. They see actual sin as the discrepancy between the potential for control and what actually takes place.

Dynamics of Sickness

A great deal of sickness comes from defect (what we are born with or without), distortion (results of accidents, or poor mentors, or ill-fitting shoes, or response to stress), or invasion (microbes, assaults, indoctrinations without the power to respond).

The reason we talk about a dynamics of sickness is, however, that, even when defect and distortion and invasion are present, they very seldom, alone and of themselves, account wholly for the resulting condition. The result is always affected, in one degree or another, by an internal factor that may be called "decision." [30]

My theory presupposes the basic notion that there may be "secondary gains" in illness. That is, the person's suffering may be very real, but he may also get out of certain responsibilities because of the illness. It also relies heavily on Karl Menninger's coping theory of illness.[31] The heart of this theory is that what now constitutes trouble was a pattern of dealing with life— originally, when it took form, a strong way of coping with threat or challenge. The person, saved from a worse fate by the defensive devices he employed at the time of threat, may continue to cling to them. The situation changes, but his coping devices remain the same. If he saved himself once by withdrawing, he now continues to withdraw even when relatedness would be in order for his own fulfillment. If the discrepancy is too great between his mode of coping and the actual situation now, the result is illness.

A paradigm of this situation would be the person swimming in very rough water, about to go down for the third time but near shore. Suddenly a breaker lifts him up toward the land but not upon it. As he goes by, he manages to grab the limb of a tree. There he clings, actually saved in fact but of course exhausted from his effort and the panic of his near-drowning. Hours pass, the sun comes out, the waters recede, and all should look very much better. But our friend, at least metaphorically, still hangs up there on the tree limb that has saved him.

Suppose that, years later, we approach him for an interview. By this time he has plausible reasons for making his life in the tree. We ask him if his situation does not make various things, such as marriage, a bit difficult. Or if his isolation is not distressing at times. Or why he scorns the beautiful sand only six inches beneath his feet. Or would he like to go where he can see television?

His reply to us will be a wonderful rationalization. He will extol the merits of trees, demonstrate how supple he is from hanging on, interpret his isolation as appropriate privacy, ignore the question about the sand at his feet, and decry television. At least, he will do this if his coping has not been accompanied by too much hurting. If he hurts, he may be more open to a reinterpretation of his situation.

Without the initial capacity to adapt himself, in the face of great threat and with a paucity of resources, he would indeed be dead long since. But, having endured serious threat or challenge, he has hung on to the patterns that enabled him to cope with the threat, despite their increasing irrelevance. He is indeed chained to his past. Special effort will be needed to get him out of that tree without his having a collapse in doing so.

Whatever he is, however, he is not just weak. What he has entombed is strength. He did catch the limb and cling to it and was thereby saved. It is no wonder that he has clung to what once saved him decisively even when, from other perspectives, this clinging is irrelevant. The person trying to help him to come into the modern world does well to recognize his strength and build on it. Nothing happens if he is simply seen as up a tree. If he is yanked from the tree and put in a good hospital, his panic might kill him despite the new comfort.

I agree with Karl Menninger that this is the general paradoxical dynamic nature of sickness when it cannot wholly be accounted for by bugs, breaks, and defects.[32] In theory, the man on the tree limb could at any time have looked at the sand, the waters, and the sun, and concluded that he no longer needed that kind of refuge. Most of the time, most people are able to do just that in spite of threats in their past experience. When one cannot do so, he becomes like the man on the tree limb and needs special help.

More in the background than in the foreground with our tree-clinger is the factor we have called decision. We do not know, over the years of clinging, how many insensitive people came along to make fun of him, or to tell him how fine the weather was, or to try to pull him down. The probability is that there were some such people, and that our man, in order to avoid looking a complete fool, had to tighten his defenses about why he was up in the tree. That is, his needed decision to leave the tree was no doubt impeded every time he worked up a new defense for why he was there.

In this kind of situation, usually much less obvious but equally enchaining than the man in the tree, the factor of decision is clouded and obscure. It is a horrible thing for the well-wisher to comment on the warmth of the sun, the proximity of the sand, and the delights of a world beyond the tree in such a way as to shame the man for being where he is. What can enable the man to decide that it is safe to leave the tree? Only a kind of interpersonal help, generally speaking, that regards his being in the tree as representing initial strength.

Any voluntarism that approaches the man in the tree with a simple and common-sense invitation to be sensible and climb down is sheer nonsense. Needless to say, I would disagree violently with the observer who decided that nothing could be done except to leave the man to his branches. I think the best helper would leave the man in the tree until a certain stage in their dialogue had been reached. He would be equally concerned to let the man see that his being in the tree was the result of genuine strength, but that his tree-existence should be evaluated in the light of the fact that there is no longer storm or threat of drowning. The helper would believe all along in a potential capacity for decision-making, but he would not try to force it. If the man came down from the tree carrying a cane, the helper would not deprive him of the cane. There are many places in the world to which one can go with a cane that are barred by hanging on a tree limb.

Exactly how much sickness, whether the symptoms be physical or mental or both, is like that of the man on the tree limb, is a subject for research. Some is and some is not, but in varying degrees. As epidemic types of sickness are increasingly brought under control, it appears that more than half of even physical illnesses now contain elements like that of the man in the tree.

A great deal of sickness comes, originally, from outside

sources over which the person, at that time, had no control.
But it seems that an increasing amount of sickness emerges as
the residual of relatively successful efforts to cope with severe
threats at earlier stages of life. Thus there is a mixture of fate
and freedom, of decision and doom, in a lot of illness. The
outcome seems increasingly to rest upon the expertness of
potential outside interveners if they are given any signals about
the need, and thus upon the capacity of the persons to recognize the need and give such signals.[33]

A Footnote on Demons

Much of the history of demon theory has plainly been detri-
mental to an understanding of sickness and suffering. The pro-
jection of the causes of mental illness and other conditions into
alleged beings wholly outside ourselves served for a long time
to deter research into the actual causes, and also gave warrant
to much inhuman treatment of the sufferers who, because of
their demon-possession, were regarded as having lost their humanity.

Although recognizing that demon theory eventually became
the worst enemy of humane understanding of the mentally ill,
I believe that a different and more basic intuition about demons
is offered in the New Testament.[34] Paul W. Pruyser, in reading my original manuscript, has warned me at this point. He
believes that my interpretation of demon theory in the New
Testament takes insufficient account of the harm that this
theory did, at least later on. In my revised discussion, I shall
take account of his warnings.

In the New Testament stories, the first point made is that
the demons come originally from outside. In *that* time and
culture, such an assertion meant that the one possessed is not
merely perverse. I think there was an early intuition that the
problem could not be dealt with by merely blaming the person. Whether it was imps or cultural patterns that began the
trouble, it did begin, in the fashion of "original sin," from
outside.

The demons then enter the person and, in the modern

sense, are coped with in some way, successfully or otherwise. So long as the person knows what is himself and what is the demons, he can make it. In the story of the Gadarene, for instance, the man bound in chains answers Jesus' question about his name by saying, "Legion." [35] That means a thousand. But a man who can say that a thousand forces are at work within him has some capacity to recognize a core of himself that can, with whatever pain, still stand aside to survey the thousand forces. This is not a cure, but it is good coping. And no matter how unclear the way, it shows that essential integrity is still present.

The third point is that there is still confusion inside. Even if the sufferer has an intuition about his own integrity despite the invasions from outside, he is still tending to mix up himself and the demons in a great state of confusion. If help is offered to drive out the demons, therefore, he does not quite know what to make of it. He is not sure who *he* is. Thus, the Gadarene shouted to Jesus, "What have I to do with thee?"

At that point in the story Jesus is reported to have commanded the demons to leave. I believe there is a modern equivalent to this procedure, but it is not in terms of a verbal command. It is working to get the psychic defenses down, to convey our belief in the residual strength of the person, and to cool it off so that not all has to be done in the next ten minutes.

Carl Jung and Paul Tillich and, most recently, Rollo May have all suggested that we need to take a new look at demons.[36] Demons are not completely evil or satanic, said Tillich. They are much more ambiguous or ambivalent, so that our understanding of their message and our dealing with them on the basis of that understanding is the factor of critical importance. Jung believed that the demon carries a message we need to hear and assimilate, not being ruled by it, but not ruling it out of our perception and hearing either.

Whatever dire things happened to demon theory after the New Testament period, and there were many, the social function of the theory at that time was to get people to realize that persons might be afflicted by forces beyond their own powers to remedy and should therefore have concern rather than condemnation. The person who did not answer a greeting might be aphasic rather than antisocial or nasty. In this sense, the New Testament version of demon theory was, I believe, a precursor of the modern conception of mental health. My friend Paul W. Pruyser does not, so far as I know, agree with this judgment.

Sickness and Repentance of Sin

Let us get down to cases and consider the attempts to help a very obese man.[37] We assume that the physiological and pharmacological means of help have been applied and recommended as relevant to this man's condition. Those measures may accomplish much, and may indeed solve the problem.

But let us suppose that, in our man, there is more, as is often true. We would hope that his doctor, then, would work toward the goal of getting him to realize that he had been trying to get something important and legitimate (such as affection or security) by means quaranteed to defeat the end, and to produce other troubles besides. If this realization should come, then the man would be relatively open toward being responsible for his future condition. At least in relation to his overweight, he would have been convicted of sin, and would have found the power to repent.

As a second illustration, let us consider the patient in long-term psychotherapy who, in his actual life situation, keeps on repeating certain pathological patterns of action in spite of the fact that his therapeutic discussions have repeatedly demonstrated such patterns to be self-defeating. On one day he may come to his therapist with a striking story of how he has "got at it." He may be both right and pertinent to the sphere involved. But his improvement in one area is no automatic guarantee of problem solving in other areas. Thus, he will still have to work on the other areas and on the problem in general. Repentance and change in one area do not automatically carry over to everything else.

The repentant sinner who believes that, once he has done the big thing, everything is easy from there on, is quite mistaken. Even after a man has passed the decisive point, said Martin Luther, he is still *simul iustus et peccator*, that is, still both righteous and yet a sinner at the same time. We must be properly grateful for the experience that has meant change and advance. But we must not over-generalize it to mean that all is clear sailing from there onward. Luther put this matter in terms of coming always, again and again, to Jesus Christ.

What do we do when, despite our best efforts and those of our helpers, it becomes apparent that the roots of our sickness will remain recalcitrant? Whether we began too late, or the causes were too early and too deep, or the secondary gains were too inviting, what happens when the chance of constructive change is very small? There is no real answer to such a question except doing our best to acknowledge our participation in mortality. At such points of life, repentance means, I think, getting rid of perfectionistic notions about what life means, and settling down for what is best within what is possible. Perfect functioning has disappeared. If we can repent of our unqualified desire for it, then quite often the functioning that is left contains many possibilities for creativity.

If everyone had precisely the proper degree of conviction of sin, he would not thereby be made perfectly healthy. But within his limits of health, such a conviction would enable everyone to maximize his functions and his creativity. Hence, the conviction of sin, as appropriate, affects health in the sense of optimal possible functioning.

Sin and Sickness

Within the limits of space, the story of the relationship between sin and sickness, a very complex one, has been given. We now summarize.[38]

The first summary point is to warn against all crudities or over-simplifications from any side about the relationship of sin and sickness. It is not so long ago that one was sinful if he turned up with tuberculosis, and the man today who has an ulcer or a heart attack is threatened with a blameworthy judgment even though sin is quite otherwise from that. The fact is that sin and sickness are related and not related in very complex ways. Most of the old saws are wrong. But on closer analysis, and with a truer understanding of both sin and sickness, there are profound relationships. Since sin is not a message of doom but one showing where we can take hold, this is not a bad but a good finding. It offers more opportunities for us to exercise freedom and get well.

As a footnote to the warning about over-simplification, we do well to note that our affluent age has produced an increasing number of people whose principal preoccupation seems to be protecting their health. If you are a physician, you must do what you can to protect health. But if you are anyone else, and even perhaps if you are a doctor, you may well wonder about this person who dares have no social concern because it might raise his blood pressure, or no involvement with other people or institutions because it might prove ambiguous and get him worked up. By the values to which I adhere, such a person is misguided, stunted, or narcissistic. Whether or not we call him sick is a matter of terminology. Perhaps sickness is the wrong term, since he could change his view.

The second point is that the conviction of sin, in the positive sense in which both the tradition and I have presented it, does not come about easily. We cannot get people to see this and that about themselves, however patent it is to us or others, if we simply bore in and accuse. The one chance of bringing it about is to supply a context of support and understanding but also honesty of dialogue and response. That means no reluctance to serve as supporting, or father, figures when that is needed.

Finally, just as sickness is not simple, so I think we must agree that sin is not unambiguous either. I firmly believe that God is more interested that people repent of sin and change their direction than that they be found sinless by some heavenly auditor. When I say sin is ambiguous, do I mean that it is partly good? In terms of final effect, I certainly do not mean that. Sin is evil and has evil consequences. But a sinless man would have no awareness of sinfulness and might therefore be less than human. Since sin is a part of the lives of us all, therefore, the question is not whether our sin is good or bad (mostly it is very bad), but whether we can see its meaning, repent of it, look for the aid we need, and move ahead.

In the first chapters of Genesis, Adam and Eve are shown to have "fallen" into sin. It is no contradiction of this teaching about the fall to allege, at the same time, that they rose into the necessity of dealing with the ambiguities that are inherent in all actual human life. Anyhow, their fall was qualified because they brought out of the Garden of Eden some revelations that have not lost their meaning with the passage of time.

What is religiously important about sin is not that somebody, we or our forefathers, did bad things. Of course they did and we have done so too. It is that the decisions of human life, even when they turn out badly, are not above repair if they are seen within the context of the God who unambiguously wills the fulfillment of mankind so long as he does not have to remove man's freedom in the providential process of assistance.

Chapter 5
CHURCH AND COMMUNITY

The title of the present chapter was not a part of my original lectures at the Menninger Foundation. In those lectures I was trying to find the closest and clearest points of kinship between theology and psychiatric theory, so that the psychiatrists, psychologists, social workers, and others who were present could profit in an optimal way from theological insights no matter what their personal views on religion.

When James Luther Adams read my first manuscript, he was generally kind about its content and method, but pointed out that I had so emphasized the concern of theology with personal types of relationships as to obscure its equal interest in social and institutional relationships. This critique has been held in mind in the total rewriting of the manuscript, and the reader will find something about society and institutions, as well as persons, in every chapter.

It also seemed wise to introduce a new chapter focused clearly around the larger kinds of relationships. In this area I have less wisdom than in relation to the other topics. But a writer cannot evade crucial aspects of his subject.

There will be no basic change of method in this chapter. The aim is still re-examination of theological ideas and insights in the light of knowledge from the psychological and sociological disciplines, or reappraising theological doctrines from a dynamic point of view.

The discussion will begin with the doctrine of the church. Whatever else the church may be, it is the primary social institution that thinks theologically, teaches theology, and tries to practice the insights it possesses through its ministry and service. Since it exists to serve God and not itself or merely its own members, it has concern for all mankind since all are equally God's creatures. Therefore, we shall add a discussion of theological understandings of community to those about the church.

Church

There are *three metaphors about the church* that have been of major importance in the two thousand years of history. Like the metaphors already discussed in understanding the dynamic meaning of sin, each of these has tried to say more by its analogy than ordinary discourse would permit, and each metaphor has, similarly, tended to emphasize some factors more than others.

In one important respect, however, the metaphors about the church have differed from those about sin. Each metaphor about sin emerged at a different period of history, and one rather than the others tended to be a better interpreter at particular times. I have argued that all the sin metaphors are still relevant if reinterpreted, but did acknowledge that one metaphor seemed to have more appeal today than the others.

In contrast, the metaphors about the church have all been on the scene from the start. To be sure, there have been many shifts in the ways in which they are interpreted. Some groups in the church have tended to use one metaphor at the expense of the others, and other groups have used a different metaphor.

Today these historic preferences are far from disappearing. And yet with the rise of ecumenical relationships there is a much greater tendency than ever before to see merit in those metaphors about the church which have not been used traditionally by one's own group. A dynamic analysis of each metaphor seems to me to offer a wider and deeper range of understanding of the church than would have been possible in past ages. But this belief must not blind the discussion to the way in which these metaphors have often served as channels of division within the church.

The first metaphor is that which sees the church as the *body of Christ*. It comes directly from the New Testament letters of Paul and was his favorite (but not exclusive) way of referring to the church.[1] As Paul himself developed the idea,

109

it contained three principal features. First, Jesus Christ is head of the church, and is related to us in a way similar to the relationship between a head and a body. Second, because Christ is head of the church and inherently related to the church, it follows that we are all organically members one of another. Third, each person who is in the church is needed in the same way that every part is needed to make an organism function. No one need be ashamed of the part he plays in relation to the whole.

If we were to encounter for the first time this analogy between a social institution and a biological organism, I believe we would be struck by its intuitive wisdom. Set aside are, for instance, mechanical notions of relationship within the church. Not even in the name of God or of Jesus Christ are men to look only upward and fail to see the kind of organically interdependent relationships they have with one another. Also set aside are political or power notions of relationships within the church. Jesus Christ is indeed the head, but there is dignity and meaningfulness for every member. And the kind of headship exercised by Jesus Christ is in no way a dictatorship. He is presumed to know more and will better for the church and its members than it or they can do for themselves. But he simply requests them to fulfill their functions. He does not use force to compel them.

The body-of-Christ metaphor becomes, in some respects, even more cogent when considered in the light of later biological findings that Paul did not have at hand. Like any man of his time, for example, Paul knew nothing about homeostasis, the process by which the fluids of an organic body are kept at proper proportions despite even severe threats from the outside. Failure anywhere in the system of dynamic interrelationships will produce death. Thus, Paul's stress on the important place of every member within the total body is given new credence in the discovery of biological homeostasis.[2]

Another point that Paul could not have known is that headship or leadership in an organic body can be understood only in terms of the development of the body through various stages.[3] In an embryo, for instance, control of form by particular parts is determinative up to a certain point, but from then on, a larger center takes control, and any part that is out of line at that point becomes a permanent impediment. If Paul had understood these processes, I think he would have realized that co-operation with the head, Jesus Christ, becomes more important as time moves on, but that the earlier stages where headship is more divided are necessary in the total process.

It is not necessary to my argument that every new biological discovery give Paul more reasons for his understanding of the church as the body of Christ. In balance, however, I believe that most of the crucial discoveries reinforce Paul's intuitions about organic life: its complex interrelatedness, its need for all its parts, and its possession of some kind of head that values the parts and does not conspire to get rid of them.

If this metaphor of the church is so sensitive to the significance of every member, and so positive about the organic nature of the member-to-member relationships, and so non-coercive about headship, then we may well ask why it has not become the metaphor above all others.[4] The fact is of course that it is wide open to distortion. Jesus is no longer here as a human person; so headship at the human level must be humanly debated, dealt with, or seized. Every part or person is essential to the whole, but leadership may decide that it knows just what each should do, and declare the other sinful if he does not do it. The whole idea of the body of Christ may be interpreted as solidarity of idea, group, or ritual, so that holding the body impermeable becomes the total goal. In such a situation, the church shortchanges its duties to the rest of society, fends off new insights, and assumes a basically defensive stance, in order to protect the "body of Christ." Such a body is, however, no longer truly organic. It has frozen so many parts, and so distorted the relationships of parts to whole, that it would no longer work as a literal organism. With the instincts of a magnificent therapist, Pope John XXIII lured the Roman Catholic Church out of its particular kind of preoccupation with a debased body-of-Christ view of the church.

When Protestants came along, they were very sensitive to the misuses of the body-of-Christ metaphor of the church. They tried to diversify headship at the human level through pastors and elders and deacons and synods and assemblies. In order that each member might truly contribute to the whole body, they translated the scriptures, commended scripture reading to families, and instituted pastoral work that went out to the people. All these were good moves, but the unhappy fact is that Protestants generally gave little attention in a positive way to the body-of-Christ metaphor of the church. They associated it mainly with those aspects of Catholicism against which they were testifying, and thus let it lie instead of reforming it.

I believe that the body-of-Christ metaphor of the church is deep in its intuitions and worth saving, for Catholics and Protestants alike. But the dynamics involved in the metaphor must be more clearly delineated and the distortions more clearly judged than has been true in the past, if this eventuality is to occur.

How can we save it? The first step is, I believe, a recognition that the center of the metaphor is about our human interrelatedness and not about who or what is to control it. Headship, whether by popes or vestries, must be carried out with the best possible checks on arbitrary power. We now know enough about forms of democratic government to realize that there is no contradiction between an effective and strong executive branch and controlling legislative (and judicial) branches. If we get the leadership question settled sensibly, and leadership becomes more responsibility than privilege, then the great merit of the body metaphor is our realization that we work in organic interrelationship, and that is our strength. Fights will still go on, as in a way they do in a bodily organism. But if there is still commitment that is widespread and not coerced, then the church really can be like an organism in basic respects. Parenthetically, we might add that the church's reconsideration of itself, and of its theology, is very much like the feedback processes without which organic life would not be possible.[5]

When mainline Protestant Christianity arose in Europe, the second of the three principal metaphors about the church became prominent. This was the understanding of the church as a *covenant community*. Protestants took their warrant from the Old Testament covenants between God and Israel. The basic features of the Old Testament covenants (they were not all precisely alike) were that God offered to do certain things for the people on condition of their doing certain things in return, that God did not exact strict legalism in observance by the people but would show mercy beyond the letter of the law, and that the covenant was itself made by God in his love for the people and therefore he would be forever concerned with the people even if they failed in their part of the contract.

The early Protestants were suspicious of the body-of-Christ metaphor of the church partly because the headship of Jesus Christ seemed to have been translated into political terms and exercised by the pope and his aides including priests, and partly because the organic relatedness seemed to be understood as a compulsory community endangering human freedom.

Engaged in search for a metaphor that would guarantee against such errors, they lit upon the covenant idea from the Old Testament and modified it. The church exists, they held, because God called it into existence. It was a result of his initiative, not simply a human idea. Its human forms and powers and structures were never to be held as beyond criticism, any more than its members were to fancy themselves as beyond sinfulness. But by extending his covenant to the church, God has declared special concern for it both as an institution and for its members. As with the earlier Jews, there is an obligation on the part of church and members to live up to their part of the covenant, or, when failing, to come to God in Jesus Christ and ask forgiveness.

As against the then prevailing interpretation of the body-of-Christ metaphor, the strength of the Protestant covenant community analogy with the church lay in its emphasis on human responsibility about carrying out its side (not assuming that things worked automatically if everybody belonged) of the covenant, in its emphasis on the sovereignty of God who offers the covenant because he loves mankind and not because he has to do so, and in the realism with which power was

113

dealt with at the human level, acknowledging it but devising forms to check up on its use.

In actual institutional practice, the covenant idea proved to be capable of just as many distortions as had the body-of-Christ metaphor. Each group could regard itself as participant in a special covenant, the content to be specified by it, and ruling out the content of alleged covenants between God and other groups. Thus the growing sectarianism was partly brought about by the way this metaphor was used. Furthermore, how was it to be decided when a group was or was not living up to the covenant? Many groups were too sure that they knew the right answer and penalized those they regarded as offenders. The Puritans and the Quakers got a lot of flak for their protests against then current covenant doctrines. But translated into freer ground, they mostly did to others about what their oppressors had done to them, some small exception being made for the Quakers. The Mennonites too had learned something about tolerance.

If the great metaphor of covenant is to survive and be creative, there is one point of the dynamics that must be addressed seriously which has had scant attention in the past. This is the fact that covenant involves promises, and that promises are limitations of choice in the future in the light of the present.[6] The use of covenant theory to limit arbitrary powers has already been noted and praised. Also lauded has been its function in increasing both individual and corporate responsibility within the covenant structure. But a covenant, like a contract, binds some factors about the future in order to preserve, in both the present and the future, some values or relationships that are felt to be worth this limitation on future freedom. If you contract to marry one woman, you cannot (unless serial monogamy wins out) marry another, at least within a reasonable time, and without dealing decently with the first.

If the church is a community with which God has established a covenant, what does that mean for God's freedom in the future? The dramatic story of Jesus Christ indicates that God did not confine his covenant with the Jews to the earlier means of saving them (or mankind), like the escape through the Red

Sea. So covenant doctrine must not mean that God is committed only to the means he has tried before. Believing in his benevolence, we see nevertheless that he may try new means either to cement the covenant or to help those who have broken it.

Promising has also, however, to do with human beings. If they approve their part of the covenant with God, to what extent is their future foreclosed, or to what degree is the future still open to new insight and even negotiation? It is not true to suggest that all human beings in some way break their promises. Some human beings and human groups hang on tenaciously to their sides of the contract, resist information that would call for a change, and obfuscate all chance for new vision by their clinging to chapter and verse. Promising may be evaded, but it may also be overdone.

In the light of modern dynamic knowledge, the question is whether the church has regarded promising and covenanting as simple possibilities requiring only a verbal declaration, or as difficult and ambiguous decisions needing a great deal more than votes or vows or affirmations. Because promising is basically a cutting off of certain decision potentialities in the future, in favor of values regarded as basic for both present and future, I believe that it always has inherent ambiguities and difficulties. Except in unusual instances, these problems are not paralyzing. Decision is still possible and on good grounds. But unless promising is to be reduced to the primitive level of the child who, for good and sufficient reasons, promises thereafter to "be good," there needs to be something more than assentive grunts and declarations.

Promising is a responsible way of dealing with the future in the present. Or it should be. While not dispensing with the ability to use freedom in the future, it nevertheless makes its declaration on certain values believed to be important in the future as well as in the present, and thus, whether it knows it or not, it reduces the range of future freedom. Buy a house with a mortgage, or even a car with installment payments, and the point becomes clear.

Except for the work of Herbert Schlesinger, still unpublished, there are virtually no dynamic studies of promising. Schlesinger's work is monumental, but until it has been published, it cannot be quoted. I fear that some aspects of the previous discussion may have unintentionally plagiarized Schlesinger, but I hope not. His own treatment of promising is so rich that my small comments at a dynamic level, while owing much to his unpublished work, are nevertheless only an introduction to his analysis.

Insofar as the church is a human community that has accepted a covenant offered by God, with assurance on God's side of mercy as well as legal justice, it can make some kinds of promises but be wary of others. What the church has usually done, whether Catholic or Protestant, is to try to attain present security by closing off choices in the present that would affect the future, or open it up. To make a promise is to assume some kind of power, admitted or not. If we promise or covenant to do something we believe God has asked for, our acceptance of the covenant assumes that we believe we can do it. That is, that we have the power to do it.

The fact is, however, that conditions change. When we signed the mortgage notes, we saw our way clear. But interest rates change, and so does our income, perhaps in the other direction. There is no point in promising that is exempted, on ethical grounds, from dealing with the new situation, whatever it happens to be. Purely legal contracts have no such flexibility. But covenants, in the religious sense, must have it. The covenant metaphor is, therefore, immensely helpful but only if we understand its dynamics and its temptations to distortion.

The third metaphor about the church also came to us through the New Testament as the *household of God*.[7] Whereas the base of the body-of-Christ metaphor was biological, and that of the covenant metaphor was mutual contract plus mercy. that of the household-of-God metaphor stresses relatively intimate interpersonal relationships. We should be wary lest we read into it the modern nuclear conception of the family containing only parents and children. The household of God clearly meant an extended family. A principal point made by this notion was that everyone who is in it at all belongs fully.

God has adopted us into his own household. This concept was, then, peculiarly powerful in its appeal to people who felt cut off.[8]

Even though some use has been made of the church as the household of God by nearly all groups, the metaphor has taken a commanding position among most kinds of movements attempting renewal, or fighting a rigid ecclesiastical structure, or seeking a new kind of joy in their faith. Anton T. Boisen examined the emergence of several such groups during the past century and this one and pointed to a series of phases through which they tend to go.[9] First there is the great excitement of new spiritual power. Those who felt left out before now feel that they belong. There is much singing and other evidences of joy, and at times cultivation of what are felt to be special blessings of the spirit including phenomena such as speaking in tongues. At first the new groups have little awareness of the larger institutions of society; theology tends to be more emotive than reflective, and therefore the household of God makes a great appeal. As Boisen noted, they eventually have to learn how to create leadership, to settle disputes, to raise money, and to get along after the initial enthusiasm has passed; so that eventually they tend to become more like other churches.

The springing up of new groups trying to revitalize faith has been characteristic equally of Catholicism and Protestantism in the West. Most monastic orders began in this way, and so certainly did the Franciscans. The precursors of the Protestant Reformation, the Anabaptists, were in this kind of tradition. In their case, and that of some other groups, the household-of-God metaphor led them to confine the powers of church government to the local congregation, a position which of course had to be modified as the need arose for missionary work, for an educated ministry, and other things.

The special dynamic contribution of the household-of-God analogy about the church is the stress on belongingness. Whatever one's condition, or whatever be the rest of society, in God's household we become his adopted sons and have meaning.[10] But since this contribution is most needed just by those who otherwise feel most estranged, the temptation is for such groups to remain ingrown. Very often they have used criteria for like-mindedness in a legalistic kind of fashion. When they survive, as in the case of the Franciscans or the Baptists, they tend eventually to make much more use of the body-of-Christ and the covenant metaphors.

In discussing the groups that have relied mainly on the household-of-God metaphor of the church, we have noted their tendency to treat power questions by fixing them in the local congregation or face-to-face group. The tendency of those following mainly the body-of-Christ metaphor was to have a hierarchy of power from the top down. Those chiefly guided by the covenant metaphor have tended to have a balance of powers. I would hold, however, that these alignment tendencies are in no sense inevitable, but represent sensitivity to some kinds of concerns and yielding to temptation about others. There is no inherent reason, if the metaphor is analyzed dynamically, why the church as the body of Christ needs to be organized hierarchically, none why the covenant analogy churches should be so fearful of power that they fail to allocate enough authority to do the job, and no reason why the churches relying on the family-of-God metaphor must be so fragmented as to lose influence in the world. If the dynamics are understood, and the temptations fully realized, then each metaphor has at least some contribution to make to all groups.

Brief mention may be made of three other metaphors of the church that have had a wide influence, among many additional ones that have been used. First, the church has been seen as the *communion of saints*.[11] The intention here was not to claim special virtue for those who are in the church, but to thank God because he has made fellowship possible, and to see one's being in the church as a movement toward holiness even if such a condition is never achieved. Another intent of the analogy was to provide a sense of history, our communion with those who have gone before. The temptations of this metaphor are so obvious as almost to require no comment. People and groups can become smug, thanksgiving turns into privilege felt to be deserved, and the whole group may become more ingrown.

Another metaphor used was that the church is a *school*—or,

to bring it more up to date, a kind of *hospital-school*.[12] Here, the church as healer and guide was in the foreground. Being in the church does not exempt one of such needs; therefore, the intent was to have every Christian be appropriately humble about having needs, and diligent about continuing his education through his whole life. As it was actually used, there were two big temptations in using this model. The first was that the schoolmaster, or the pastor, often assumed authoritarian methods of going about his task. The second was that there could be such concentration on the inside care of members that the larger society, other men, and institutions would receive little notice.

The final metaphor to be mentioned here is either the *leaven or yeast* that works in the bread, or the *fire* that needs to burn when there is rigidity or stagnation.[13] In other words, the emphasis of this analogy is on the church as having a special mission to the whole community or society. By conceiving its task as service beyond itself, bringing the good news to all men who will receive it, it should guarantee against focusing on the in-group. In practice, of course such a strongly missionary view of the church has sometimes meant presentation of a too narrow faith, rejection by those outside, and a consequent compensatory conclusion that it is right and others are wrong.

With these three last metaphors about the church, as well as with the three discussed previously, my thesis is that all can be drawn upon constructively in understanding appropriately but critically the nature, meaning, and function of the church in the world. My argument has been that dynamic analysis of each metaphor helps to reveal both its strengths and its temptations, and that, therefore, the more penetrating the analysis, the more likely we become to use any metaphor constructively without getting bogged down in its temptations and lapses.

Church and Community

From the beginning, Christianity had to deal differently with community from the way Judaism had done. At first a

119

small movement among Jews, it quickly decided that Gentiles were equally welcome to the Christian community. Since Judaism as a whole did not look kindly on this new movement, both Jews and Gentiles who joined it had to find their main identity within it. That meant for them all various degrees of break with their previous community identities. The earlier Jews had considered community as coterminous with their nation, even when in captivities, and even though they had wars among themselves. Thus their community was given, and centered and focused in their religious faith. They had international relations with other peoples but not community with them. When Christianity arose and included both Jews and Gentiles, the question of inner community was settled by understanding the church. Men could enter the church no matter what their previous communities. But how, then, would the church deal with the rest of society, with communities not a part of itself? [14]

The first answer was given by Jesus himself in his teaching about the kingdom of God. He treated this paradoxically.[15] It is both something that we now have within us in what modern language would call an attitude and a spirit and a mode of relatedness. But it is also something to come on a larger scale in God's own time, but toward which we can work.[16] The clear implication is that God wants the kingdom to come to all men. Indeed, this is the basic gospel or good news; so that the people of the early church set themselves, in thankfulness to God, to bring the good news to as many as would receive it. Such actions meant diligent missionary activity. For several decades after the death of Jesus, the church, like all the renewal and new light groups that were to follow it in Christian history, concentrated on cultivating the new faith and bringing in new members. Organization was loose. The world out there was seen mainly as a field for mission.

Not far along in the second century the church began to organize itself for more efficient work.[17] The kind of officers a church should have was specified with one person as a sort of chairman seeing that everybody got his job done. Later, in what came to be called the office of bishop, an area or district had a presiding or supervising officer also.

In this brief account it is impossible even to offer a summary of the next astonishing stages in the relation of church to community. The church was persecuted; there were defections from it, and after the persecutions it had to be decided whether people could be permitted to return. Suddenly the world became not just a backdrop for the work of the church, but a serious potential enemy. The movement began that was later to lead to monasticism, withdrawal from the world in order to protect the integrity of faith, and often of course also to render service. Then came the astonishing transition when this hitherto small but growing group found itself the official faith of the Roman Empire. From being persecuted to being chaplains to the rulers took only a short time in the long sweep of history. It is small wonder that the understanding of the relation of church to community has had a checkered history.[18]

As societies became more heterogeneous, the churches had to deal with two fundamental aspects of their relation to the community. The first was about power, focused on the relationships of church and state but also including the power of economic and other social institutions. The second was about how they should interpret their mission of service to the world not only by direct service but also by participation with other social institutions in working for the human welfare of all mankind.

On the power questions, one or more churches have at some time taken nearly any position that can be conceived.[19] They have blessed a state and related institutions, tried to withdraw from contact with them, tried to control them, attempted to have two or more separate realms of life, and have taken other positions as well. Even when power has been exercised so inhumanly as under the Hitler regime, part of the churches yielded to that although of course other parts, at great cost, refused to do so. And sometimes they still live, as in early Christian days, under persecution.

Paul Tillich tried to bring some theoretical order out of this chaos of practice by suggesting as the basic principle that the use of power is always to be for the ends of justice, and to the extent that this is done, love in the theological sense is at work.[20] This way of putting the matter is especially important in asserting that the churches cannot bypass the issues of power, either their own or that of other social institutions, and have at least the obligation to use such power as they have or can affect to increase justice as they best understand it.

Since the churches may be at fault in their understanding of concrete situations, and since there are likely to be disagreements within them, the next clear step seems to be democratic and representative discussions leading to majority views but without disrespect for those of minorities. Inefficient as it may sometimes be, this conciliar system seems the best we can devise to meet ever-changing situations. The Second Vatican Council was a striking breakthrough in this direction. If there are effective discussion and dealing with power at the policy level, there is no reason why the churches cannot be more efficient in their work through strong executive leadership if it is finally under conciliar control.

When a church through good information and competent discussion has reached a majority view on an issue where power and justice are involved, should it use its power of persuasion to try to have social powers used toward the ends of justice? The most widespread, but not universal, answer today to this question is affirmative.[21] Within most churches, however, there are sizable groups that want the churches as churches to keep silent on such questions, and to have only individuals speak out. If the churches should adopt this latter atomistic view of relationships within the church, then they would be presupposing that the church itself is not the kind of body that can or should be concerned with the use of power to increase or decrease human justice. In its primary intent, none of the six metaphors about the church which we examined can support such a separation between church and community.

At the present time there is a striking difference in the degree to which churches in the free world can use their power of persuasion toward the ends of justice, and the limitations confronted behind the iron curtain. But there is no cause for relaxation in the free world, whatever may occur in the Communist countries. We still retain a lot of freedom to speak.

But the problems are so massive—Vietnam, race, pollution, the cities, housing, and poverty—that some genuinely new ways of using power for the ends of justice may have to be tried. Against such possibilities, or even their advocacy, the system itself may prove to be the most immovable institution of all. Another demand that our complex situation makes upon us is that we know in detail what we are talking about.

We have a growing number of theological leaders today who have enough knowledge of social and institutional dynamics on how the church can best help power to be used in the interests of justice. My own knowledge of such sociodynamics is limited. But I know enough to believe that if the issues are interpreted in the light of the sociodynamics, the general directions in which power should be exercised will become clearer to more people and more churches.

The other side of the church and community relationship is about the mission of the church itself to the needs of the worldwide community. The first question was how the church deals with other social institutions like the state to move in the direction of justice. But the church has, without apology, also a direct mission to the world as well as an indirect one. As in the first century, it still has the obligation to bring the good news to all who will receive it. But this cannot be a mission of preaching and words and worship alone, crucial as those are to the gospel. How do we minister directly to human need as the Good Samaritan did?

Very soon after foreign missionaries went out from the United States in the early nineteenth century, those ministers of the preached word began calling for teachers and physicians and agricultural workers as well. As time went on, more and more of the missionary outreach of the church was in the form of bringing to disadvantaged peoples things that they needed and wanted. Then governments here and there began meeting needs they could not meet before, for example, by setting up hospitals and clinics. For some decades, missionary strategy has been concerned not to duplicate services, but to try to shift the services offered and the places in which they are rendered, so as to give maximum help. That process still goes on, at home and abroad. In terms of the total need, of course the amount of such services is small.

There are some in the church today who tend to decry or at least regret services of this kind. They argue that the real task is of using the power, at least of persuasion and perhaps more, to get fundamental conditions changed, and that relief operations here and there may obscure the enormity of the need. I am certainly in favor of better roads and street lights and police that might have prevented the Jewish victim from getting robbed on the road. But it would seem to me disastrous to rule out of the church's responsibility any obligation for Good Samaritan work.

In a very introductory way, I hope that this chapter has demonstrated some of the dynamic factors involved in the way the church is and can be understood, and also a bare beginning at guidelines on the relation of church to community.

Chapter 6
SEXUALITY AND LOVE

In each of the five preceding chapters, the leading title word has been clearly about something recognized as a classical theological doctrine: freedom, grace, providence, sin, and the church. In the present chapter that continuity could have been maintained by making "love" the first title word, for there is a Christian classical doctrine of love. If that course had been followed, I should have been tempted to treat sexuality as an afterthought or at least very briefly.

"Sexuality" has been put first in the title not of course because it is more important than love, but to convey my conviction that there is basic Christian teaching about sexuality, regardless of how much it has been clouded or obscured. "Love" must of course accompany it, for that is the context in which the Christian understanding of sexuality appears. Because of space limitations, however, the treatment of love will be brief. This decision about procedure runs some risks. But it seems important to take those risks in the light of the rapid shifts of sexual attitudes and behaviors in our society.

As suggested in the title of this volume, I have tried to show in each of the previous chapters that a dynamic approach to each of the teachings increases our understanding. Is there such a dynamic, a mixture of tensions and equilibrium, also possible about the Christian teaching on sexuality? My answer is yes, and the principal elements of the dynamic will be shown as an earthy acceptance of our biological nature, on the one hand, and a conviction that God is working through sexuality toward spiritual ends, on the other hand. Clearly, there are also dynamics involved in our having two sexes rather than one, and in the many dilemmas that arise from the interaction of strong sexual desires and the needs for social control.

THEOLOGICAL DYNAMICS

I shall begin with the biblical understanding of sexuality and try to establish from it something like a basic theological teaching, not exempting this view from criticism by modern dynamic insights. There will be a truncated examination, next, of the development of sexual attitudes in theological history. A basic set of principles for understanding sexuality theologically today will then be set forth. At the close, the discussion will elaborate the context of love in which theology finds sexuality to belong.

The Biblical Understanding of Sexuality

The Old Testament view of sexuality arises from the doctrine of creation. When God had completed the original creation, as the story is told in Genesis, he looked upon everything and judged it as very good.[1] This judgment included his having made men and women, Adam and Eve's looking upon each other naked and not ashamed, and Eve's function, as the story puts it, to be a companion or helper to Adam and not merely the mother of his children.[2]

What God has made, including man's animal nature, is to be accepted and enjoyed, its expression guided in some ways rather than others, but with no notion that things of the body are in any way inferior. This position made the Jews very earthy about sexual behavior. But since sexuality was made part of the creation by God himself, it was also believed to be "sacramental" in nature.[3] That is, something of the holy, before which one feels both lure and awe, is contained in sexual experience itself. Sex of course was not the only way in which God worked through material means for sacramental ends. But because of the very emotionality inherent in sexual relationships, the sacramental idea was especially relevant in this realm. Modern scholars believe that the very ancient Jews, like some of their neighbors, practiced something like temple prostitution for a while, as a primitive way of dealing with the holy. But anything of this kind had disappeared on ethical grounds by the time of recorded biblical history.

Throughout the Old Testament, the combination of a completely earthy realism, along with a constantly refined conception of the sacramental, is to be found. The early forms were crude. Stories like that of Samson are nothing to trust young people with if we want their sex education to be all refined and delicate.[4] As time went on, however, crudities were cleaned up without destroying the realism. Monogamy became customary after the early polygamy. Moves were made in the direction of acknowledging women as persons. In stories like those of Jacob and Rachel, affection becomes more important.[5] But even though historical development brought some refinement, the basic principles remained unaltered in essence.

We should beware of interpreting the earlier customs like polygamy as simple evidences of license for males. First in nomadic society, and then in agricultural communities, many kinds of controls had to be strict or the people would have perished. For the Jews this reality was reinforced by the various captivities they had to undergo. The early Jewish way of handling domestic government was very patriarchal. With this approach, and in the conditions of the time, and with women for a time regarded as property, there could hardly be such a thing as an unattached woman beyond some part of the teen years. Even the ancient injunction that, if a man dies, his brother is obliged to marry the widow, is an indication of this same situation. That was what confronted Onan, for instance, who apparently did not like his brother's widow or at least did not want to support her, and he is reported to have spilled his seed on the ground.[6] Against later moralistic interpretations, the story had nothing to do with masturbation. If Onan's seed had found its way into the widow, he would have been married to her, fulfilling his obligation. He was condemned for his social irresponsibility.

If a man had sexual relations with a woman who was not the wife or concubine of another man, and not a close blood relative, they were, in effect, married. Wedding ceremonies should be thought of not as making the relationship all right by vows, but as public acknowledgments. Indeed, in such a culture where living arrangements made privacy unknown in the modern sense, sexual violations must have been difficult to carry out without detection unless one had the power of a king.

In early Jewish society there was no adultery when a man had sexual relations so long as the woman was not the property of another. He was of course required to take care of her, unless he decided to divorce her. Divorce was strictly a one-way street, a husband having the right to get rid of a wife. Life must have been very grim for a woman so discarded. We do not know much about how the ancient Jews looked on masturbation in children, but the very absence of mention in the Bible suggests that it did not disturb them. Incest is mentioned often in the Old Testament and is always strongly disapproved.[7]

In relation to homosexuality, there are only about six clear-cut references to such practices in the Bible.[8] It is clearly condemned but in general terms. D. S. Bailey believes that the most famous reference to homosexuality, when men outside Lot's door try to have him release his guests so they may "know" the men, is not in fact a reference to homosexuality at all.[9] Other scholars disagree.

It may be an exaggeration to say that early Jewish sexual morality was based less upon sexual factors than upon the rights men had in their female property of wives, concubines, or daughters. But the story leans in that direction. In Judiasm at least until the time of the Essene sect near the start of the Christian era, there was no hint that a virtue existed in refraining from sexual relationships.

By the time of Jesus, Jewish marriage had become generally monogamous, there was increased social criticism of a man who threw out his wife and thus divorced her, and advances had been made in acknowledging women as persons. When Jesus spoke sharply against divorce, the context shows that he was condemning that conception of personhood that could permit a man at will to eject his wife.[10] Similarly, his comments on adultery seem to refer more to broken personal relationships, or interpersonal irresponsibility, than to the formal Jewish definition of adultery involving the rights of males. Except on such points about personal responsibility, Jesus said very little about either sex or marriage, except for his prophetic critique that even marriage might stand in the way of finding fulfillment.[11] His concern was, however, with remaining open to the kingdom of God, and there is nothing he said that gives any warrant for an anti-sexual attitude.

The extensive New Testament comments on sexuality and marriage are by Paul. Since Paul lived a relatively long life and remained a bachelor against general Jewish customs and clearly did not like the Hellenistic libertinism that was so much a part of the Mediterranean world of that time, his comments on these topics have usually been interpreted as negative. Such an interpretation cannot be set wholly aside. Paul expressed the wish that other Christians might be as he was, maritally unattached.[12] He conceded that it might be better to marry than to be preoccupied and unable to think of anything else. And when he wrote beautifully about the attitudes of spouses toward each other in the letter to the Ephesians (which however Paul may not have written), he was mainly concerned with using marriage as an analogy of the relation between Christ and the Church.[13]

Yet there is one long and astonishing passage in Paul's letters, the seventh chapter of the first letter to the church in Corinth, that is both more profound and more positive about sexuality and marriage than anything else he said. The reasoning is also better and more subtle.[14] At the time Paul wrote that letter, modern scholars believed that he expected Jesus to return within a few years perhaps within Paul's own lifetime. Such a return would mean an entirely new world and the disappearance of this world. Hence, Paul was thinking about what Christians should do in this supposed interim period. Later Paul, along with other early Christians, realized that the timetable had been wrongly set.

If it were a simple fact that Paul was an advocate of keeping away from sexual and marital relations whenever it could be managed, and that sexuality was probably tainted anyhow, then we should expect his writing on this subject to begin and end with an exhortation not to get involved if you could help it, and let it go at that. It is true that this exhortation is

129

given at the start. But what is astonishing is what comes afterward.

Some people had been married before becoming Christians,
and some of their spouses had not followed them into the faith.
Paul tells them two things. First, if continued testing shows
that you cannot persist in the faith and remain married, then
you may feel free to separate. Second, try, nevertheless, to
remain in the marriage, for it may be that this intimate relationship can be used by God to bring your spouse to the faith.
My conclusion is that, despite his single-minded concentration
on the new faith, Paul was still a Jew in his interpretation of
sexuality and marriage, but his sense of urgency made him
ambivalent about any other possible loyalties than the new
faith.

The net effect of the ambiguities in Paul's position, however, has made it possible for many groups in Western Christian history to appeal to him when they wanted to denigrate
sex or marriage. The fact that appeals have been made to Paul's
position does not of course mean that their understanding of
it was correct. Eastern Orthodox Christianity, for example, although it has had monks, has never required a celibate priesthood. When this latter plan was adopted in Western Christianity, however, as universal in the tenth century, of course
some appeal was made to Paul. We must admit, however, that
Paul's ambiguities have stood there for two thousand years for
anyone wishing to appeal to them.

With the exception of the partial ambiguities in Paul, and
granted the movement from crudity toward ethical sensitivity
in the biblical understanding of sexuality and marriage over a
period of time, the twin basic principles of regarding sexuality
in an earthy and realistic way and at the same time as a part of
God's sacramental work in the world are together what define
the essence of the biblical approach.

Unless you have some very special reason, do not scorn what
God has ordained: including your physical needs, your need
for companionship, and your obligation to contribute to the
next generation. Sexual expression is not necessarily essential
to a full human life, especially if you have a great commitment

requiring concentration of energy. But even if you were Paul, there would be no warrant for believing that you would be better in God's eyes in refraining from sexual expression as an inherent mark of virtue. Controls over expression are indispensable. But there is no merit in suppression as such.[15]

Historical High Spots About Sexuality

In spite of the generally clear, although not cloudless, witness of the Bible about sexuality, some odd attitudes have been taken in the history of Western Christianity. Our purpose in this necessarily restricted discussion is to mention a few of them, suggest how they came into existence, and then frankly analyze them. Not everything between the Bible and the modern era was wrong or a lapse from the biblical view. There were advances, as we shall indicate. But we cannot understand the history at all without taking seriously the distortions of the biblical understanding.

In radical contrast to the situation in Judaism, the Mediterranean world to which Christianity first extended itself was full of sexual libertinism. Indeed, as shown for instance by a non-Christian Hellenistic author of about that time, there was even a kind of sexual athleticism.[16] Jewish Christians were repelled by such views and practices. As Paul's first letter to the people of Corinth shows, some of the prevailing Gentile libertinism crept into the early church under the guise of Christian freedom.[17] Paul felt it necessary, therefore, to define very early and sharply the unacceptability of such views. But individual persons, when they became Christians either as individuals in the early centuries or later en masse when the empire adopted the Christian faith as official, had to struggle with this dimension of their general environment. There was often deep personal conflict between the two views, as Augustine made clearer than anyone else.

Celibacy as a requirement for clergy in the West did not become mandatory until the tenth century.[18] And the reasons for it then were not so much anti-sexuality, although that was present, but were protective of the ecclesiastical institution by having no loyalties that might compete with it.

THEOLOGICAL DYNAMICS

The story of the rise and fall of monasticism in the West is long and difficult. The movement began with individual hermits and flagpole sitters, fleeing from the world for various reasons including the obtrusiveness of sexual matters. By the fifth or sixth century the individuals had given way to groups. Until the sixteenth century, the monastic orders, and later the friar groups as well, became the most distinctive feature of Western civilization. It is well known that the monastic orders preserved learning during a period when much of it might otherwise have died. It should be known more widely than it is that monasticism in the West was nearly always involved in social services, helping those who needed help in realms such as illness or guilt. The Franciscans and Dominicans made important contributions, but they were far from the first to hold themselves to ideals of service. Ironically, some of the pre-Franciscan orders got themselves in trouble by being too diligent. They raised more than they needed, sold it, became rich, and lost the early zeal.

The monasticism of Eastern Orthodox Christianity, which has never had a celibate priesthood to go along with it, was, by contrast, relatively unconcerned with the social services that might help illness and poverty. That monasticism was, at least sociologically, much more like that in Hinduism or Buddhism, where also a few people were set apart to cultivate internal life and pay as little attention as possible to the peoples around them. Western monasticism was always busy tilling the fields or aiding the people, at least until it became rich enough to get drunk.

I continue to puzzle about the dynamic meaning of sexuality to monks in the Eastern tradition, who could have married if they simply wanted to be priests, and to monks in the West, who had had to remain unmarried in any event. The Eastern group cultivated their own insides, their own spiritual life, at the expense of social concern, as shown even today in the depleted monasteries of Mount Athos in Greece. The Western monks did what they could about advancing their own spiritual life, but they were also in the monk business to try to help the needs of people around them. Peter Hartocollis, an American psychiatrist of Greek background, reported after a recent trip to Mount Athos, once a great and large community of Christian male Eastern Orthodox monasteries and now rapidly dwindling, that the atmosphere was so dominated by anti-sexuality that even female birds were to be kept off the island if at all possible.[19]

The dynamics of these differences are very difficult to get at. In the West, both priests and monks had enforced celibacy. In the East, one could be celibate as a monk but, if he wished, married as a priest. Yet the monks of the West were founders of social services, while those in the East were not. My very tentative guess is that monks in the East were, as a group, more turned in upon themselves psychologically than were monks in the West. Thus, as a group, they may have been evading people more than sexuality. But all this is speculative and hypothetical, however interesting. Perhaps the reason why Eastern Orthodox monks were socially unconcerned comes from cultural and not from religious sources.

If one asks flatly how much the renunciation of sexual expression was involved in the development of Western monasticism (as contrasted with the East, where it was plainly a large factor), the answer is difficult to find. Some of the monks whose writings are available to us clearly relished their sexual temptations even when giving themselves merit badges for setting the temptations aside. A great many others realized that sexual expression is not essential to a full human life, and went on with their respective commitments of worship and service and learning.

Nevertheless, even if this is Protestant bias, I am compelled to say that what made possible such a huge development as monasticism became in the West was the underlying conviction, on the part of many very good people who wanted to do their best, that God could be served better if there were no close human ties. Marriage was not denigrated for those who needed it. But if you really wanted to be somebody before the Lord, then you renounced it.

What emerged slowly but finally and fatally was the underlying conviction that the unmarried person served God in a superior fashion. Thus, not engaging in sexual relationships (even if socially responsible) came to be a mark of merit before God. In the New Testament, renunciation of marriage had been like that which Paul describes for himself (he may of course have been concealing motivational data), namely, to get on with the job, even if some sacrifices are required in the process. But when the merit system, i.e., that celibacy is better liked by God on inherent grounds, became fixed, monasticism and eventually the general clerical celibacy of the West became a special way of serving God. By this time both the Jewish heritage and the Bible had been left far behind.

Since monasticism is a major threat to the view of sexuality on Christian grounds that has been advocated here, if it is regarded as a special merit in the eyes of God, it is especially important to see that monasticism, whatever its virtues and vices in actual practice, acquired its connotation of anti-sexuality as a by-product and not as a principal motivation.

If one lived in the tenth century or in three or four more later, if he were not a part of the nobility, if he were not sufficiently dominated by his aggression to join the military (there were few full-time military jobs anyhow), if he had brains and wanted to do something with his life more than tilling a small plot and living on the edge of starvation, and if he had also a concern to help other people cope with life—then he had no other choice but to go into the church's orders as priest, monk, or brother. Eventually he would have some other options as the universities got underway. But it would be a long time before he had any viable option but a church vocation if he wanted to serve God and also get out of the mess. Along with a decision in favor of cultivating his abilities, he was of course presented with the merit system. No wife, on any account. But: thereby God blesses you more.

The conditions of family life throughout the Middle Ages were nonprivate in the extreme in all classes of society, even the nobility, and were very primitive for all except the upper class.[20] Even so competent a critic of our modern technological society as Lewis Mumford tends to go romantic over the late Middle Ages.[21] But I do not believe he could stand those actual nonprivate conditions of the Middle Ages any better than I could.

Even in noble houses, a great deal of the service was performed by children from other noble families as well as by those from lower class families. A child who could be placed in a large household hardly rebelled, for the home from which he had come was nothing but a one-room shed with a dirt floor. It is hard to imagine any child of the Middle Ages who had not more than once witnessed sexual relations on the part both of his parents and others. It was the rule rather than the exception for children to be exploited sexually as well as in other ways, often only by teasing them but sometimes also in overt behavior.

As Philippe Ariès has shown, the very notion of childhood developed only from about the time of the Renaissance and onward.[22] Before that, the child went through six or seven years of infancy and dependency, and then went to work. The history of painting, as Ariès demonstrates, shows that only very slowly did children get the right to wear clothes appropriate to their energies and their interests. In such households, rich or poor, how could one ever get a spot of privacy? Or freedom from watching sexual relations in the same room? For a long time, the one answer was monasticism in some form.

But social institutions had begun to change. Nationalism was in high gear, trade had increased, and manufacturing had become a profitable business, a new middle class was emerging, and options were appearing for the male that were new. Higher education had increased, although it was still small by modern standards. All these changing factors in society enabled the Protestant Reformation of the sixteenth century to challenge the contention that those people who are dedicated to celibacy are better in the eyes of God. So they went back and forth between their understanding of the principles and the actual sixteenth-century situation, and drew from their reflections the conclusion that anybody could be celibate and a good man if he wanted to do that on his own, but that enforced celibacy in order to please God because it was alleged to be a better condition deserved no aid or comfort.

Martin Luther, himself a monk, took his own wife from a nunnery. Marriage, he said, was a natural part of the life God intended for most people, and sexuality in marriage is therefore good. If some people did not want marriage, or could get along without it, fine. The one thing they could not do, however, was to declare themselves better before the Lord for being unmarried or sexually uninvolved. Except for regarding sexuality as something for most people to be dealt with in a marriage relationship, with God's wholehearted approval, Luther had no other special insights about it. He ignored or dealt lightly with the problems we have in our day; hence he cannot be literally quoted about them. But to have moved from monk to married man, and with a nun—how much can we expect from any human being even with Luther's genius?

Contrary to their undeserved anti-sexual reputation, the Puritans were not Puritan about sex when it was exercised in the marriage relationship. Like the ancient Jews before them, they were concerned about children with no fathers to support them, and they did not have the "out" of polygamy. So they developed a scarlet letter, a poor coping device against the wrong person. But they were much more realistic about sexuality, at least in marriage, than were the Victorians who were to follow them.

In the United States of America, I believe that the hypothesis about our frontier, especially during the nineteenth century, does much to account for the distortion of the Christian understanding of sexuality as found in the Bible.[23] As the frontier moved west over several decades, the two centers of the life of each new settled community became: the church and the saloon. The saloon always had a fixed location. The church, if in the hands of Baptist farmer preachers or Methodist circuit riders, might take a while to assume architectural form. Hence the saloon had a geographical lead.

If you were on the frontier, in its early stages especially, you usually associated with one of the town institutions but not the other. If you went to church, you heard a good deal about what you were not to do. If you dared to risk the saloon, you encountered loose women who, even if their motives were mainly financial, came to symbolize sexuality. Since persons on the frontier had many offspring, they clearly engaged in sexual relations at home. But the fact of such activity was kept as quiet as possible, because of the association of sexuality with the women at the saloon.

Something about the morals and customs of those frontier communities later became stylized into the pattern of the western motion pictures and television shows. The villain was shown as trying unsuccessfully to get the good lady school teacher. The hero fended off the villain satisfactorily, but he usually closed by riding off into the sunset rather than marrying the girl. Even in their more sophisticated versions, these shows are nostalgic hankerings after a world in which the morals are black and white. The frequency of violence in them is a corollary part of their appeal. Sexuality is seldom dealt with in anything like a mature way.

It seems likely that this frontier background, when added to the general Victorian tendency to keep sexual matters hidden, had much to do with the fact that no Christian theologian published a forthright book on what the Bible said about sexuality until the 1940s.[24] There were many discussions of marriage, even a few indications that the sexual relation in marriage was a good thing although that point was sometimes not explicit. But it remained for Otto Piper to say what should have been evident to scholars for a long time, that the Bible takes a basically positive view of human sexuality.

I am sure that most Puritans, Victorians, Frenchmen, Italians, Englishmen, and Germans all along had no qualms about sex in marriage as being in accord with the will of God. But the peculiar ways in which each society has dealt with sexuality, usually with a considerable discrepancy between its stated standards and actual behavior, shows that part of the problem has been fear of accepting the basic biblical understanding that sexuality is good both because it is earthy and because God accomplishes his purposes partly through it. To be sure, the exercise of sexuality is not to be done without some conditions being set. But Western societies tended to hedge on the most basic point. Dynamically speaking, refusal to accept human sexuality as inherently good in God's eyes led to too narrow conceptions of its meaning, and also enabled some of the worst distortions to go on unchecked by the stated ideals.

In attempting these historical high spots about attitudes toward sexuality in Western theology and life, I have tried to suggest some of the complex factors, often not sexual in nature, that have produced the major distortions from the biblical understanding of sexuality as rooted in creation itself. Some of the conditions that produced the attitude distortions have now changed. There should, therefore, be a new opportunity to understand the basic biblical view of sexuality, and along with modern dynamic knowledge, use it to set forth constructive Christian approaches for our day.

The forces that have produced distortion, however, are not dead. For example, a report entitled "Sexuality and the Human Community" was submitted in the spring of 1970 to the General Assembly of the United Presbyterian Church.[25] This report took a positive position toward sexuality on theological grounds, and also discussed many current moral questions in the light of its basic position. The Assembly did receive the report and sent it out to the churches for "study and appropriate action." [26] It also approved the basic intent of the report in this phrase, "believing that Christian faith affirms sexual being as a God-given dimension of life to be used for the creative intent and purposes of God." [27]

But it added, under pressure from the minority opposition, "reaffirm our adherence to the moral law of God as revealed in the Old and New Testaments, that adultery, prostitution, fornication, and/or the practice of homosexuality is sin." [28] There follow some wise words warning against mere condemnation of sinners. But it is far from clear that what the biblical writers meant by the terms, especially adultery and fornication, is the same as the meaning assigned by the framers of the above statement.[29]

This chapter is too short to permit of anything but mere mention of the question of progeny and the population explosion which is a very severe threat to the world and about which not much is being done. The immediate issues are about contraception and abortion. In a recent study of Protestant statements on contraception in this century, I was surprised to find that genuinely forthright statements in its favor appeared only in the 1950s, long after the practice among Protestants had become general.[30] This makes me a bit more optimistic about a future shift in official Roman Catholic attitude, since the practice is growing rapidly among Catholics. But since practice changes most slowly in underdeveloped lands, that is where the immediate tragedies will be greatest.

It is becoming more and more clear, however, that there is little likelihood of arresting the population explosion at any tolerable level through purely voluntary measures. Such means could of course be easily abused, but that danger will have to be faced if voluntary efforts do prove insufficient. In this respect, there is no precedent in world history, and we shall have to explore our heritage not for direct statements about progeny but for principles about the value and nurture to human beings.

A Constructive Theological Understanding of Sexuality for Today

The starting point for such construction lies in the basic biblical understanding of sexuality as good both because it is part of our basic equipment as organic creatures and because God works through it for spiritual ends. The Presbyterian report already mentioned sees the second point also as "an instrument of God's reconciling activity" in that, rightly used, it is a "vehicle of the spirit and a means of communion."

Theology needs to be equally against the two opposites of the above position, first, libertine or exploitative views of sexuality, but also, second, a debasing of sexuality so that it cannot perform its God-intended functions. The tradition was right in its concern for the first although often wrong in its frequently legalistic way of approaching the subject. But the tradition has tended to speak only lightly about the second, the debasing of sex as if it were a subhuman kind of concern.

In what follows, I shall present briefly a summary statement

139

of constructive principles for today, with some modifications from a similar statement published earlier.[31]

1. *Since God has created man as a sexual being, and since man is also a whole being and not a mere aggregate of parts, sexuality is good if it serves the fulfillment of man as a total being, that is, if it serves the will of God for man.*

2. *Man's total self or being (spiritual or organismic) has its very existence in the community of other selves, and it is the proper aim of all human interrelationships in all their aspects to foster the love in which spiritual or organismic selfhood is nurtured. Sexuality is one of those important aspects.*

3. *The developmental aim of sexuality in human life is toward a progressive integration of the several necessary levels of sexual purpose or function: biological, psychological, interpersonal, and spiritual.*

4. *In human life, sexual relationships are understood to need both intensity and steadfastness, and a proper relationship between the two, if they are to fulfill their function. Both intensity and steadfastness are needed to foster love and communion, and they ought not to be set against each other.*

5. *The meaning and good of any sexual act or relationship are always dependent in some significant degree upon their inner meaning to the persons involved. But since sexuality has social dimensions and consequences, and is ultimately to serve man's fulfillment according to the will of God, the meaning and good of any sexual relationship are finally to be evaluated by both criteria and not by either alone.*

6. *As in relation to all other dimensions of life where responsible decisions have to be made, the aim of the church is to foster, as appropriate to age and other conditions, an optimal capacity for responsible decisions that are based on a firm grasp of the basic Christian understanding of sexuality combined with an informed and responsible grasp of the factors in the actual situation. Approaches through law or rules, when they seem necessary, should never displace attention from the primary task of developing capacity for responsible decision.*

I have tried to state the above principles so that they would be intelligible to the reader of the preceding material without further commentary. They begin from the biblical basis as I understand it, and each point has a reasonably clear connection with that basis. They draw, however, upon modern dynamic understandings of the nature and pathologies of intrapsychic, interpersonal, and social and institutional forms of relatedness, since sexuality exhibits all such dimensions.

Since the focus of this book is on a dynamic approach to several theological doctrines and teachings, this is not the place to try to show how the principles enunciated can help us with our views and attitudes on complex sexual problems in society: contraception, abortion, population control, homosexuality, sex education, prostitution, trial marriage, divorce, marriage preparation, and much else. In forming views on all such topics, and even more in guiding people toward forming their own responsible views, many kinds of specifics have to be put into contact with the principles. And I am sure that my statement of principles can be considerably improved on. Nevertheless, statements of this kind may perform a significant function. They are "middle principles" between the "Christian ethic of love" and the complexities of all actual situations.

Theology and Love

The Greeks of the classical period had a typology of love which, except at one point, is difficult to surpass. First came libido, or sexual love which might or might not have friendship or other higher things attached to it. Next came philia, love in terms of friendship, where there is mutuality and exchange. We give and we get. We need and are needed.

Third was eros love. Today we think of the "erotic" as the sexual, but eros had a more comprehensive meaning. Eros was the love that is aspiration, like the creative absorption of the musician in his music, or the love of the man and woman that is so satisfying that each is stimulated to reach out to other satisfactions in nonsexual realms. Eros love may also be love for one's country or the world when he wants to make the nation or the world the best it could possibly be.

The Greeks had also the word "agape" for love, but they

141

used it loosely. Only in the New Testament did it acquire a special kind of meaning.

That meaning was, in a general sense, that agape is the love that seeks no reward for itself or no mutuality of return. It was used mostly to try to describe the love of God for man. It has often been called sacrificial love. Is man capable of agape? About all the New Testament tells us on this question is that any agape capacity that man may have is only derivative from God's agape, and is not a human possession.

According to the most careful and informative account of recent years, by Daniel Day Williams, there is no effort in the New Testament to confine love to agape, in the sense that libido, philia, and eros could be forgotten.[32] The agape dimension of love should deepen the meaning of sexual relationships, make friendship more significant, and guide us in our aspirations, and thus make our loves into some kind of unity. But it also seems clear that trying to understand love without taking agape into consideration distorts the situation. If libido, philia, and eros, singly or together, declare themselves to be the whole of love, they must be refuted.

In most Western theological history, the issues about agape have generally been of two kinds. In the first situation, it has been assumed that there is a genuine relationship among the forms of love including agape. But it has then been asked whether man is in any way capable of agape love, even if he has come into the church through Jesus Christ. Since the agape love comes from God alone, through Jesus Christ, it is not man's possession or his ability. Therefore, can he speak of it at all in relation to himself? If he does so, is that evidence of the sin of pride or hybris?

The other question about agape has been more practical than theoretical. It has assumed that love is as love acts. If one has received something of God's agapic love, what is he doing about it in consequence? The paradigm for this question may be Francis of Assisi, a rich man who became poor and went about doing good. He tried to pass on the agape love that he believed had been given to him.

In modern times Anders Nygren has argued that agape in

the New Testament is so unique that we cannot assume it as related at all to the other forms of love.[33] Most other theologians have regarded Nygren's position as extreme, not only because it tends to take agape out of the realm of human life altogether but also because it makes no explicit provision for relating agape with the other forms and dimensions of love in actual human life. Williams argues convincingly against the Nygren position.

The position of St. Francis that love is service is something that nobody can deny outright. But as the world has become more complex, it is not so easy to be sure about what is and is not real service in the sense that Francis intended. In today's world, low income may be as much a mark of servility as of genuine service. And a man who earns enough to support his family is not necessarily failing to be of service even in the Franciscan sense.

For the modern world, the main theoretical question may will be whether love understood in a sacrificial sense has positive meaning, or is simply pretension or denial or even a kind of masochism.[34] When sacrifice is genuine, the loss that is included is a by-product and not part of the intention. To be sure, the element of loss may be in the mind, as in the swimmer who tries to rescue a child but finally drowns. Nevertheless, if a person in that situation should recover, he would feel that he could not have lived with himself if he had not made the effort. I do not like to think of sacrifice as "doing one's duty," for that carries overtones of legalistic acquiescence perhaps to the Superego. But the sacrificial action of the man who plunges into the water to save the drowning child involves risk and concern and, temporarily, a suspension of how one is going to come out.

Perhaps sacrificial love can be understood as a form of risk-taking, a kind of gambling although not for profit. The situation poses problems of potential and even fatal loss. One rises, equips himself for the emergency as best he can, and plunges into the metaphorical water.

It is misleading to allege that sacrificial love has no self-motivations. It chooses among its values, whether in crisis or

143

other situations, and acts in accordance with what seem to be the higher values. When the situation demands, according to its value system, it risks even the physical self, as in the swimmer trying to rescue the child. But it makes no sense to say that such effort is heedless of self. The swimmer wholly heedless of self is not exhibiting sacrificial love but unconscious efforts at suicide. In genuine sacrificial love, the self is transcended for the purposes of action, but it is not laid aside as of no value.

In the Christian understanding of sacrificial love, the paramount element is action that follows from character that genuinely cares. Human beings may change their stance at the last minute in view of pressures, but the model is the constancy of God's love. We cannot guarantee that God might not change his mind, but if our faith has meaning at all, it is that, on such basic matters, he does not change his mind or intention. Therefore, the astounding Christian declaration that God sent his only Son into the world, finally to be slain for the salvation of mankind, declares God's intent to sacrifice for higher values. But it does not imply that God felt the loss was greater than the gain, nor that he or we should mope about the losses rather than giving thanks for the gains.

At the human level also, genuine sacrificial love flows from character, and the last thing the persons who demonstrate it think about is that they are sacrificing. I recall a cartoon of parents, confronted by friends, cooking a mite of pemmican over an open fire in an otherwise unfurnished living room and admitting, in response to questions of the guests, that the education of their children cost a pretty penny. Since they did not seem emaciated but only inconvenienced, the cartoon showed them as sacrificing without feeling it as sacrifice, that is, as choosing some values over others.

The important fact about sacrificial love is the existence of a character that must be exercised when the situation calls for it, beginning with the man jumping in to rescue the drowning child. Different people do possess this character in different degrees, and their readiness to risk cannot avoid being related to their technical proficiency, i.e., how good they are as swimmers. Thus, the action of sacrificial love is a combination of character, skill, perceptiveness about danger, and readiness to act if the action is not sheer foolhardiness and the danger is real. Whatever sacrificial or agape love may be, therefore, it is not mere rash act. It is sober conclusion, after reflection, no matter how quick, to act with such and such risks ensuing. Action of this kind, when it appears, may very well be the closest human action approach to the divine. But it does well to be preceded both by reflection on the principles and concrete analysis of the actual situation in light of the principles.

There is no question that agape is a component of love in actual human life, although it is always imperfect and always intertwined with the other dimensions of love. Giving a case on this point is risky but worth the trial.

Years ago I sat in on a case conference at the Topeka State Hospital when Karl Menninger was serving as consultant. The background was discussed, and then the young woman of about thirty entered the room and sat with Karl Menninger at the head of the table while the rest of us looked on. He talked to and questioned her very gently and intelligently and very humanely for a while. And then she asked him, "Do you remember that I met you before?" He did not remember and honestly said so. Then she told of an occasion, about two years before, a Thanksgiving Day when she had been disconsolate. She had been wandering over Topeka, and had sat down in her misery on a bench near the Menninger Foundation head-quarters. She said, "You came by, sat down, and gently talked with me. I told you a lot that day. And even though I am now a hospital patient, I shall never forget what it meant to me to have you sit down and talk to me on that day, especially your noticing me and sitting down—and on Thanksgiving Day."

I do not know what this recollection meant to Karl Menninger, but it was very meaningful to everyone at the case conference. Suddenly the technical and the human sides of psychiatric relationships came together. The agape part of Karl Menninger, whatever other parts there might be, had brought together not only for the patient but also for a whole group of staff and students the dimensions of love at least as appropriate to a psychiatrist and his patient, and perhaps a good deal beyond.

Psychiatrists know a lot about the libido and the philia dimensions of love, and they are in process of learning more about eros, the love that involves aspiration and commitment and promises. But not enough of them, or of any of the rest of us, are prepared to sit down on a bench on Thanksgiving Day as Karl Menninger did at least that year. It is a great fact that professional persons like clergy, psychiatrists, and others have got themselves equipped as well as they could to help people who need help. All the same, nobody can say at breakfast, "I am going to emit agape today." All he can have is the readiness. The situation must supply the need.

Although respecting and wholly approving agape love when it can in some degree be brought into actual human living, my argument has been that love in the Christian sense is represented not by the appearances of agape alone but by the appearance of a merger—to use the old Greek categories which are hard to beat—of libido, philia, eros, and agape.

I would deny flatly that sexuality is wholly to be subsumed under libido. Sexuality should also lead to and derive from friendship. It should have aspirations and be ready to support them. And sexuality, if it is responsible and realistic and not mere selfishness, should have some agape dimensions also. If any one of these dimensions is cut off, sexuality in its basic meaning is also shortened or impeded.

When theology asserts that sexuality can be understood only in a context of love, a complex assertion is being made that cannot be met by simple moralisms. Sexual behavior does not in itself guarantee a movement toward love. But sexual relationships that do not move toward increasing both intensity and fidelity are suspect.

Christian views of the relationship between sexuality and love have historically been mixed. Even our brief account of some historical high spots shows why "sacred" and "profane" love were frequently put at opposite poles. As Roland H. Bainton has shown, it took a long time in Western history for the romantic and the companionship dimensions of marital relationships to be domesticated.[35] Before that process was well under way, perhaps only three centuries or so ago, it is true that sexual relationships even in marriage might often appear crude, and with no apparent kinship to agape love in the Christian sense at least beyond a mother's early care of her child. Today, whatever the problems in our romantic view of marriage and sexual relationships, and they are many, it is nevertheless not so difficult to see that love at the libido level should be linked with love at the other three levels, even though it requires work and not mere passivity to move in that direction.

Chapter 7
DEATH AND COURAGE

The understanding of death is one of the most complex and thorny questions in the whole of Christian theology. This fact is partly owing to the wide gap, in nearly all ages, between theological views and popular piety. It is a truism among cultural anthropologists that customs and ideas about death are always the last to change as a society changes. Christianity succeeded only in part in changing the views that the converted peoples possessed beforehand, first around the Mediterranean world and then also in northern Europe.

In addition to the discrepancy between the learned and the ordinary people, however, theologians in all ages have hesitated to tell the whole truth. Even though the Old Testament does not set forth the notion of an immortal soul, and the New Testament makes a clear distinction between resurrection of the body and immortality of the soul, it is only in modern biblical scholarship that these points have been made clearly, and even then not by all the scholars. One such scholar, Oscar Cullman, has reported receiving more protest mail from his work on this subject than on all his other writings put together.[1]

Once the question is asked seriously about the dynamic forces that have made virtually all popular piety and most theological scholarship distort the biblical understanding of death, the answer is not difficult to find at least in general terms. When any culture comes to ascribe great value to individuality and personality (no matter whether it guarantees this condition in practice), then the professed social valuing of the person's existence is added to primitive feelings of omnipotence which everybody carries (mostly unconsciously) as residues from infantile experience, and the result is that culture reinforces primitive dimensions of psychic life and gives them apparently grown-up sustenance. Under these powerful motivations, even straws may be grasped at in support of individual survival concepts of various kinds of which the Bible was wholly innocent.

Whether the restatement of the theological understanding of death that will be attempted in this chapter is more likely to be acceptable now, either to church people or others, than it would have been years ago, only time will tell. But I believe that a more positive reception is at least possible. Until about a hundred years ago, the ordinary person who survived infancy died before he or she was fifty. Today the average is about seventy, higher for women than for men. In the West, life is not so physically harsh as in the past except for the deprived groups. Therefore, compensatory views of death are not so automatically compelling as they once were. And disadvantaged groups like the American Blacks now argue with insight that they were previously forced to rely on the ideology of a future heaven in order to be prevented from getting some justice here and now. Compensatory views of death, therefore, are not merely attempts at protection of values of the people who hold them. They may also be, and sometimes have been, attempted ways of appeasing groups under bondage like American Negroes.

The miraculous achievements and promises of modern health care greatly affect modern thinking about death. Even if only a small number of people live today to be a hundred in good physical and mental health, many more persons than those who will actually make it imagine themselves to be in such a group. Not irrationally, they count on science and technology to be able to arrest the disease they may get ten years from now. In such attitudes, there may well be a mixture of wish-thinking in the Freudian sense with rationality in view of the enormous scientific advances. The net effect, however, is to render it less necessary to engage in compensatory thinking about various guarantees after death. The effect may also be to put in limbo any need at all to reflect upon death.

149

If the modern situation has produced conditions, therefore, under which the compulsion of previous ages to believe in particular forms of personal survival is qualified, then two results become possible. First, more people may become able, if properly taught, to accept the biblical view when it is brought up to date (which is clearly my intent in this chapter). But second, if the question seems less imperative than it did to our ancestors, more and more people may simply deny or avoid the question altogether, themselves dying at various times with various degrees of dignity, but more or less taking their stand on the Fifth Amendment at least about death—"No comment." The absence of a developed view about death in persons who have reached mature years might, indeed, be a matter of possible "self-incrimination." Therefore, the analogy to the Fifth Amendment may have inherent dynamic meaning and not be simply an analogical reference.

As to the concept of courage that has been linked here with death or the prospect of death, a brief preliminary explanation is needed. The usual concept corollary with death has been hope. Because of the death and then the resurrection of Jesus, Christians could legitimately have hope in their own future individually and collectively. For a long time neglected, the analysis of hope has recently been brought back to the theological scene especially by Jürgen Moltmann.[2] Hope, whether in the face of death or depression or enslavement or accidie, is of enormous importance. Hopelessness goes beyond depression to despair, and conceivably either to suicide or rash acts of violence.

"Courage" has been used here, however, as the accompanying word for "death" not because hope is not needed, but because courage is what makes hope possible in the face of obstacles. "Courage" comes from the words for heart, and from ages that regarded the heart as the complete center of life. To have heart is, therefore, essential if one is to have hope. No one can hope who is not in some appropriate way first enheartened. Since death is ultimate, I have attempted, therefore, to go back to the most ultimate concept (describing of course actual attitudes and situations) out of which any constructive element might emerge. Hence the use of courage along with death. I am all for proper hope, but courage is more basic than hope in relation to death.

Although I shall try to demonstrate that the biblical evidence is mostly on my side in relation to the position to be set forth, I cannot allege that this is unambiguously true. For in this chapter I am attempting new theological construction, and in this process there must be some "de-mythologizing." This fancy term is simply a way of talking about the effort to separate time-bound elements of an idea or belief from those that are permanently valid. Perhaps my own interpretation may be challenged by colleagues or by others. But the need for a re-constructed theology of death seems to me imperative even if some aspects of my own formulation prove to be vulnerable.

The Constructive Thesis

From the Christian point of view there is no denial that death is first a natural or organic, and eventually an inevitable, event in each person's life. Man's hope, and his potentiality for courage in the face of death, lie in his faith in God's faith-fulness, steadfastness, and benevolence toward his creation, especially as demonstrated and proved in the life, death, and resurrection of Jesus Christ, no matter how that may be inter-preted.

The faith that man's life is under God and saved by Jesus Christ despite human sin is based upon the conviction about God's steadfastness in both past and present, and thus projects itself with similar attitudes and convictions toward the future. What, from these convictions about past and present, may be averred about the shape or form of any life that may exist be-yond the fact of death? I see no answer to this question save in the beginning form of agnosticism, namely, in admitting that we do not know. But it is even more important that we realize that our faith demands our acceptance of not knowing as an appropriate condition and not a frustration. This is the point at which courage moves from faith to hope without any need to assert such teachings as the natural immortality of the disembodied soul, which Christian faith must deny.

151

THEOLOGICAL DYNAMICS

The New Testament term of Paul, the "resurrection of the body," is a symbol for man's faith in that trustworthiness of God that is exhibited in the creation itself, where God made man both as an animal and also in his own image. In uniquely Christian thought, it is also a symbol of God's redemptive activity in Jesus Christ. Indeed, without the redemptive experience it would be difficult to read what God does in creation.

Man as spirit (pneuma) is that which unifies man, derivatively from his being made in God's image.[3] All of man, including body and mind, are parts of the unity of which spirit is the symbol. Trust in the resurrection of the body (Paul called it a "spiritual body") is therefore a subtle way of expressing the trust that God will save that which is worth saving, which is inconceivable as a mere part of man.[4]

Further discussion of the resurrection of the body will be included in the next section. In this brief résumé of my own position, however, enough has been said to indicate that fidelity to the teaching about resurrection of a (spiritual) body cannot retain its meaning if it insists on attaching riders such as a guarantee that self-consciousness will be perpetuated beyond death. Rejection of such riders seems much needed to me, although much theologizing and popular piety alike have refused to do it. This is not to say that the Christian must deny the possibility of something like self-consciousness after death, any more than that he can affirm it on Christian grounds. He must simply acknowledge that real Christian faith in the face of death lies at another point. If this step is not taken, then the result is like insisting that God include certain fine print in the contract, which then in turn renders genuine faith almost unnecessary.

Courage, engendered by faith and moving on into hope, enables Christians to face death with the proper mixture of agnosticism and serenity. Such courage is never without anxiety. But the anxiety may be held at tolerable levels by the courage. Because it is supported by faith in God's steadfastness, especially as shown in Jesus Christ, the anxiety need not become, as it does in much existentialism, defiant or resentful or resigned.

As Paul Tillich saw, the Christian should have the same courage in confronting death as the Stoic, and the same agnosticism about what specifically lies beyond death.[5] But the attitude, because of faith, is entirely different.

There, in summary form, is the central thesis. I shall turn now to further discussion of the biblical views and those of some of the early theologians of the church, and then move toward the present day and further elaboration of the thesis in the light of our changing culture.

Biblical Views of Death

Through almost the whole of the Old Testament, the concern was with the fate of the nation rather than of the individual person. The patriarchs were said to be buried with their fathers.[6] The physical reality of death was confronted with complete realism. There was almost no speculation about compensations for the person, as was so prominent in Greek thought.

This realism of the Jews was made possible by their basic understanding of man as an animated body, but inconceivable as man as a something without a body. As our discussion noted in reference to sexuality, Judaism had no denigration of the body as did much of Greek and Oriental thought. Another factor that made possible the Jewish attitude was the extraordinarily high degree of identification that the person had with the nation. When this identification was threatened, particularly under captivity, prophets like Jeremiah arose to re-establish it. He told the people in exile to plant gardens and let the Lord take care of the time table.[7]

In a very few of the latest parts of the Old Testament and the books that came between those of the Old and New Testaments, there are signs that the culture of the Hellenistic age had begun to affect some Jews, and this is shown further in the Dead Sea scrolls. But speculation about what might happen to the person after death came strictly from non-Jewish contact sources, and even to this day it plays a very small part in Judaism.

Although Judaism has never been untouched by the cultures in which it has found itself, it has, fortunately, never been diverted from its central convictions on this matter. The very question about survival of the individual was not a Jewish question. When, however, it was raised by the Hellenistic culture, three possible kinds of answer could be given by Jews. The first was to have a kind of agnosticism, or even setting the question aside, in view of faith in the trustworthiness of God. The second was to speculate about a literal resurrection of the body, and Paul encountered some persons with such views.[8] The third was to adopt the Greek notion of the separability of the person into a part that dies and a part that does not. The mainline of Judaism adopted the first course, and it is evident that this view, among the three, is also closest to the constructive thesis of the present discussion, even though it does not make specific references to Jesus Christ as does my position.

Modern biblical scholarship suggests that the very first theologizing by the early Christians was about timetables and was therefore closely related to death. In their enthusiasm for the new faith those Christians, both of Jewish and Gentile background, at first thought that Jesus would return to earth literally within the lifetime of some of them. As time passed and that event did not occur, they had to rethink their understanding of this point. Fortunately, indeed almost miraculously, they engaged in self-criticism of their previous timetable instead of becoming disillusioned about the faith itself. They thus moved away from the compensatory view that some of them would never die. At that historic point, when apparently even Paul made the shift, death was accepted, as in Judasim, as a continuing and universal reality. Whatever might lie beyond it could no longer be dealt with by denying that it would come.

The significance of this kind of response to the shift in the timetable cannot be overemphasized. The survival of religious groups that set dates for the end of the world has been demonstrably low. The conquest of disillusionment is the first step, and then the admission that this part of previous beliefs was mistaken. It has always encouraged me, as a theologian, to realize that the faith itself could not have survived without radical self-questioning on the part of the early Christians of the ways in which they had previously understood the faith.

To Paul the key to death was found at two points, the event of the resurrection of Jesus, and the conviction about the resurrection of the body.[9] Like most Christians after him, Paul believed in a literal and physical resurrection of Jesus from the dead. He even went so far as to say that if Jesus had not risen from the dead, our faith would be vain.[10] It is of course my view that the resurrection of Jesus has to be demythologized as a physical event in just the same sense in which the early Christians had to demythologize their original timetable. I can see no other way of maintaining the positive meaning of the resurrection of Jesus in the future of Christianity. But it is true that most Christian theology of the past, and some in the present, has shrunk from this task.

Owing fortunately to his Jewish heritage, Paul enunciated and partly articulated a doctrine of the resurrection of the (spiritual) body. This is a very subtle point indeed, perhaps no easier to set forth accurately today with our greater semantic tools than it was with those available in his time. There is some evidence in his letters that Paul's articulation of the teaching was partly in contending with other views that he could not accept.

Prominent in the Mediterranean world was the view of man as inherently an immaterial and indestructible soul, with man's body along just for the earthly ride and eventually to be discarded without destruction of the essential man. A similar view was held in some Oriental thought, often accompanied by the idea of transmigration of souls, according to which a soul then passed into another human body for its lifetime. Although a few theologians of the West eventually toyed with the transmigration idea, it was rejected by the mainstream of thought. More theologians, however, were tempted with the view that the essence of man is separated from corporeality.

Against this common Hellenistic view, Paul's argument for the resurrection of the body had to show that bodiless man is heretical nonsense. If a body were only optional or temporary equipment, then the whole Jewish understanding of man and his place in creation would be subverted. Not only is there nothing inferior about man's body. There could simply be no man without body.

There was, however, a group of Jews, probably quite small, who were at the other extreme from the prevailing Hellenes. They believed in a literal resurrection of the physical body. Since they were Jews, they agreed with Paul that man without body was inconceivable and meaningless. But they had taken seriously the Hellenistic, non-Jewish, question about personal survival, and had speculated that the answer was God's raising actual bodies to a new realm of existence. Such a view of course meant in effect a denial of the reality of death, which Paul could not accept. Against this view Paul asserted that the body to be resurrected is spiritual.[11]

Even today there is not complete agreement among scholars about the meaning of spirit ("pneuma") when applied to the human being. Some things are clear. It is improper to speak of body, mind, and spirit (soma, psyche, and pneuma) as if they were all of the same kind. Instead, man is body that is animated. But what makes him man in the sense of his creation in the image of God is unified body and mind presided over by spirit. Spirit, then, is not another aspect of man, but is man seen as a whole. And since spirit is derivative from God, man's unity is not, so to speak, his possession. His wholeness depends upon his recognition of its source. But it would be incomprehensible to think of man as spirit without body.

Part of the reason for scholarly uneasiness about man as spirit comes from the fact that Paul, although a Jew, nevertheless was a Roman citizen and a man of much travel in the Mediterranean world. Mostly, in his writings, he uses spirit and its relation to body, as indicated above. But on one occasion he slips and talks of man as body, mind, and spirit.[12]

To assert the resurrection of the body, and to deny that this is a literal physical resurrection, Paul declared that it is a spiritual body that is to be resurrected. And, so far as we know, he had to let the argument rest with this paradoxical statement. The physical resurrection group must plainly have interpreted

Paul as simply using body in a symbolic sense. So for them Paul's use of spirit would imply merely the intangible and incorporeal. As my argument above suggests, however, Paul meant a good deal more than that you could not touch it. He meant that, since man's unity, as spirit, is a special gift of God, and its form is unknown to us, we can properly trust in God; so that all we need to know about the form is God's construction of it, which is spiritual. But even God does not think of man without a body. Not even the most incorporeal robot can be a man.

Even though there are ambiguities in Paul about death, what continues to astonish me is the very large extent to which he said no to wish-thinking interpretations of death. As noted, he presumably first believed that some people in his own generation would not die at all but would be caught up to new life when Jesus returned. That schedule did not work out. Theologizing began. There was deeper reflection, with the result that faith in God, for the future as well as the past and present, became paramount. Yet the survival question posed by the Hellenistic world was insistent; hence the formulation of the teaching about the resurrection of the spiritual body. What it finally asserted, in a dynamic sense, was that our faith in God through Jesus Christ is more important than any conceivable knowledge, except that God will surely not make us other than men. And men have bodies.

If Paul had followed through on the logic of his position, it is my opinion that he would have said that, any time the question about survival takes precedence over faith in a steadfast God, there can be no answer except distortion, and that the form of any possible survival, therefore, must and should be left trustingly in the hands of God, with complete confession of ignorance on the part of man. If there is trust, one does not have to push God into fine print.

Some Theologians of the Early Centuries

For the information contained in this section I am indebted to the work of Jaroslav Pelikan.[13] My own knowledge of the ancient languages is too rusty to have dug it up in the original. The interpretative comments are of course my own.

Three of the five early theologians studied by Pelikan— Clement, Cyprian, and Origen—moved very far away from the subtle dialectic that Paul had established, and in large measure substituted notions about survival after death for agnostic uncertainty of the kind Paul had held. Two of them, Clement and Origen, even went so far with the notion of soul that they believed human souls to be pre-existent. On only one point were they completely biblical, being against the natural and automatic immortality of a soul. But this did not necessarily prevent them from regarding a soul as capable of being given immortality through Jesus Christ. Only two of the five theologians—Irenaeus and Tatian—saw that the question of possible immortality had to have some significant no answers along with possible yeses.

Clement was much influenced by Hellenistic thought.[14] He believed in a disembodied soul that had both pre-existence and post-existence, hence it was simply in a man for a temporary period. The Christian is seen, then, as a sojourner in the world, which is not his real or permanent abode. Thus Clement was able to see the Christian as quite calm in the face of death. Noble as the serenity may be, it is based on ideas very different from those of Paul.

Cyprian verged on seeing the immortality of the soul as standard equipment but not quite.[15] Like Clement he saw the soul after death returning to its native land and resting from human labors, and being consoled for its earthly pains. He did envision the soul as summoned by Christ and going to rest with him. And he had a comforting pastoral approach. But both he and Clement tended to denigrate not only the human body but also actual human existence in an unbiblical way.

Origen, the most speculative of all the early theologians, virtually threw Paul away in his understanding of death.[16] He believed in a soul, in its pre-existence and in its return to God as its true home. He had no notion about the agnosticism concerning the form of the future that we have seen in Paul. He knew too much that is not so.

Even though Pelikan calls the fourth theologian, Tatian, a "crabbed ascetic," he was closer to Paul than were Clement, Cyprian, or Origen.[17] Tatian believed that we are to accept the reality and finality of death. We are to have faith in God, and be agnostic about what happens to us after death. Man has not a naturally immortal soul but the image of God. If man had a soul that was naturally immortal, he could be independent of God and Jesus Christ. Infinity belongs only to God. Man is limited and finite. But he can trust in God. This position is not far from that of Paul.

Holding views similar to those of Tatian, and hence close to those of the New Testament, Irenaeus was the earliest Christian thinker to make use of process and motion categories in all his thinking including that about death.[18] Implicitly, Irenaeus saw man as properly agnostic about the shape of the future after death. To him, man's great opportunity is to grow and develop. He is made in the image of God, which means more than his rationality. The focus of man's concern should be in this world, developing in himself the qualities that come from his being made in God's image, and not in trying to find out the form of life after death. Even more than in Tatian, Irenaeus held to the dynamics of the position that Paul had established.

The work of Pelikan on five of the early theologians shows, therefore, that only two out of the five had retained continuity with the subtle dialectic about death set forward by Paul in the New Testament, and that three of them, although not entirely casting aside the biblical heritage, were much more influenced by other factors than by the Bible. With this kind of record in Christian historical theology, it is small wonder that the problem has not been merely with popular piety but also with the work of theologians.

Popular Theologies of Death in America

Some very odd things have happened to popular religious thinking about death in America inside and outside the churches. Persons like myself, who want to change these views in the direction given by Paul and the New Testament, can have a chance, however, only if we understand some of the dynamic factors that have produced these distortions.

As we have seen in the brief analysis of the five early theologians, the distortion of views began a long time ago. But the special problems for America probably began in the eighteenth century. In Europe and America a study of "natural theology" took place which attempted to reason out faith from "Christian evidences" in a philosophical vein, so that faith would not be wholly dependent upon a "supernatural" theology. Whatever the total effects of the natural theology movement were, their influence upon the understanding of death was to reinforce a "natural immortality of the soul" idea more than had the "supernatural theologies" of Catholicism and Protestantism, especially because they did not have to believe everything. Faced with this view, the more orthodox theologians felt they could not believe less than their possibly heretical rivals; so that the net result was a general assumption, among conservatives and liberals alike, that the soul was not only immortal but was very likely naturally so, i.e., that God had made it so. This was one matter on which there was almost no controversy during the nineteenth century. Soul immortality was assumed by everyone from theological professors to rural preachers. If one had declared otherwise, he would have been held to believe less than even the supposed radicals did. Not until the latter part of the nineteenth century did biblical scholarship reach the point where, on biblical grounds, these assumptions might have been challenged. And it took some time in the present century before they were in fact questioned.

In the nineteenth century popular theology was made on the frontier, which kept moving continually westward.[19] For a time life was rugged. The theologians of the frontier were the Baptists who farmed during the week and preached on Sunday, and the Methodist circuit riders who went from place to place before there could be settled churches. As we have noted elsewhere in this book, there were no grays on the frontier, only blacks and whites. With the immortality of the soul idea as part of the intellectual furniture of the ministers who were without formal theological education, the frontier view of death was not really about its meaning at all, but about whether a person was taking the right course now so that, granted the inevitable immortality of his soul, he might go to heaven rather than to hell. Thus, the question of death became moralistic. Paul's resurrection of the body was read as assuming survival with the one issue being: in which place?

Although this position was more extreme on the frontier, its sophisticated counterpart in the settled east was not basically different. Some creative thinking was going on theologically, but not about death. Souls are immortal and each person had better do something to see that he goes one place rather than another, whether he is confronted with crude or sophisticated ways of getting to heaven.

In our own day the notion of a soul that is somehow immortal has been eroded among many segments of our population. There are many reasons for the fact. With some it has been guided by better biblical and theological understanding. For many others, however, the shift has been made more adventitiously: a kind of subtle materialism so oriented to the contemporary that it represses other questions, or a pseudo-sophistication that no longer considers human questions it cannot solve, or a kind of eschatology of technology under which science is supposed to get around some day to everything including death. Despite these dynamic reasons that shift many people from either a belief in or concern about immortality of soul, my guess is that about two-thirds of the American people, if polled, would still say they believe this teaching in some form. And many of the believers would not be in church.

There can be no question that American culture generally, even in the churches, has increasingly dealt with death by privatizing it and prettying it up. If the morticians were a profession, which they are not, they would have tried to resist this trend as the clergy at times, not very successfully, have attempted. As businessmen, they have mostly given the public what it asked for. Evelyn Waugh's satire on the American funeral is indeed bitter and extreme, but it is uncomfortably close to the truth about our desire to deny the reality of death.[20]

There has been only a bare beginning of studies of responses to death and anticipated death, in the work of scholars like Herman Feifel and Elizabeth Kübler-Ross.[21] But it is encouraging that the subject of death and responses to it is being increasingly studied.[22] Nevertheless, the more it is studied, the clearer it will become that a norm is needed in terms of attitudes. That consideration leads to the next section.

Toward a Joint Secular and Religious View of Death

One of the most striking facts about the modern world, especially where science and technology have been most evident, is the greatly increased controls over death that man has acquired. The management or elimination of epidemic diseases, public health measures from water supply to polio shots, better medical care and nutrition, and many other achievements are realities in many parts of the world. Longevity has greatly increased. It is also now clear that the prevention of many accidents, many diseases, the mortality of babies, and very much else rests upon the public will to activate the scientific and technical measures that are possible. Protecting human life about such matters rests no longer with factors beyond potential or actual human control. For the first time in human history, therefore, man has the opportunity to avert a very large number of the most tragic kinds of deaths, namely, those not in the fullness of years.

At the other extreme, however, we confront an actual population explosion unprecedented in human history. We have the technical means of holding down the population size, but we have not mastered the ways of getting people to use them. And as suggested earlier, we confront entirely new issues about some degree of force and power in controlling population growth. However we may proceed with details, what I am hoping for is a new kind of sense, on the part of people all over the world, of the complex relationship that exists between human life and death. Although guided by my theology, I attempt to state this situation so that men of goodwill not admitting my religious premises might nevertheless agree with my conclusions.

Here is the way such a "joint secular and religious" view would go. People should be brought into the world only when there is at least some considerable chance that their environment can provide them with the education and the relationships needed to enable them to become functioning persons in this age. Once persons are alive and here, the goal of society should be to help everyone to live out his years so long as possible consistent with the avoidance of intolerable pain or disastrous mischance. When that condition has proved possible, then death should be understood as a culmination, not without anxiety but with thanks and blessings for the life that has been lived. For those deaths that are still tragic, there will continue to be the need for special consolation. But with man's actual and potential technological powers, not even earthquakes can be blamed on God.

To the extent that social attitudes generally, and the humanity as well as technology to back them up, move in the directions indicated, it seems to me important that societies like our own develop the kind of attitude toward death and survival that has been suggested here as the normative Christian point of view. They may have to "secularize" the position. But a view of death that held to the meaningfulness of the life of man including the individual person, for the future as well as the present, and claimed to know nothing about the state of the person after death except with some kind of trust in his fulfillment and contribution, ought not to be alien to the Christian view even though it lacks the specific Christian points of reference. Most people in our time who hold views of this kind assume automatically that theology is their enemy. While I reserve the right to try to get such persons to take a look at the unique elements in Christian faith, I believe that only negative purposes are served if the areas of agreement between ourselves and them are played down.

Death and beyond death are still the ultimate mysteries. But it is surely more human to approach the ultimate mysteries with a mixture of faith and anxiety than to be bitter, resentful, lackadaisical, defiant, or simply depressed, especially if a person dies in the fullness of years. Increasingly, compensatory

163

attitudes about death should be eliminated. There is no room in the sky of astronauts for pie. Nor is the denigration of the body any longer justified in a world that can produce enough to meet all bodily needs so long as population does not get out of hand. Nobody should be hungry or without a proper life space of his own.

My suggestion is that the Christian understanding of death may help in such directions even on the part of people who may not, for good reasons or bad, accept the entire apparatus of Christian theology.

Courage and Death

Courage comes from the Latin word for heart. What does it mean to be enheartened? The very idea comes from folk biology, which even today regards the heart as the center of human functioning. That is in contrast with scientific biology, which concedes only one point to the popular view, namely, that the heart is essential. But the heart is simply a beating muscle, and has far less to do with the regulation of the organism than do the endocrine glands, the brain, and the body fluids. The idea of courage, therefore, must be traced from symbolic rather than literal biology.

In that sense, to be enheartened means movement, putting the mind and energies somewhere no matter what threatens the organism, moving ahead instead of drifting or backsliding. Traditionally, courage has also been especially associated with situations of danger or challenge, where the normal adaptations will not suffice and something new must be added. In keeping with that insight, I believe that enheartenment must always be considered in relation to crisis. If the crisis is not too big, then one may get by most of the time. But with a special or ultimate crisis, a quality is needed at a different level. That seems to be what courage is about.

Death, whether imminent or anticipated for the long future, is the ultimate crisis. To face it even in anticipation without courage is to invite the defensive devices that have already been noted, such as resentment or guilt or compensatory wishing. To have some modicum of courage is to find the ground upon which hope may build. In such situations, hope is the unproved but not irrational conviction that both the life and the death have genuine meaning. Thus it is first courage, and only then hope, that are needed always in relation to death.

From the theological point of view, courage comes from the new self in Jesus Christ that is attempting to remain in discipleship to him despite the threat. Whatever else a disciple may be, he knows that he does not yet know it all; so he is open and, by the same token, self-critical, since the strings of his harp are always going out of key.

Much about the dynamics of courage is obscure. There is no courage if the awareness of threat is absent. In that event there is only foolhardiness. But neither is there in courage self-immolating defiance of the threat. Courage involves some knowledge, some appropriate sense of the powers of the self but also of its limitations, and finally the taking of a risk that is prepared to accept the consequences. But there is much we do not know.

We usually think of courage as appearing only when there is a situation to be met to which it is a response. In the sense, however, of a cultivated capacity in the human being to deal with situations of threat or danger, courage may be more than that. The mountain climber who replies that he climbs because the mountain is there is, if he also takes the proper precautions, declaring that he is cultivating courage as a capacity even if he has to find rather special objects against which to test it.

In considering courage in relation to death, perhaps we shall have to bring back this element of venture into greater articulation. If one were sure that in dying he were going to his true home, no courage would be needed, only some form of acquiescence. In contrast, if he believed in death as nothing but injustice, then there would be defiance, and courage would be irrelevant. The relevance of courage is partly because this life is good and God has made it, and partly because we cannot know where we go from here. Courage can form the attitudinal bridge that enables us to cross over to trust in God through Jesus Christ, steadfast in the future as he has been in past and present.

Chapter 8
WORD AND SACRAMENTS

The "word of God" is the central metaphor by which Christian theology considers God's revelation to man. It implies something like speaking on the part of God and clearly listening and hearing on the part of man. It focuses on a message that God is believed to have given and continues to give, which is essential for man's salvation. That message is believed to be given in language, the most unique mode of communication known. Presumably everything essential to human salvation and guidance are contained in the word of God.

But language, whatever its virtues, is abstract in character, and man does not always get the message simply by hearing it spoken. Thus, the sacraments are an additional medium by which the message may get through to man. They bring the same message, but they operate through a wider range of human perceptive capacities. They are symbolic acts, but their form is much closer to concreteness than the verbalized message.

The thesis of this chapter is that both the word and the sacraments, and the relation between them, need to be understood dynamically if their real meaning is to be separated from possible distortions.

We have already suggested the nature of the dynamic relationship that exists between the word on one side and the sacraments on the other. If the word were left alone to bring the message, many would hear incorrectly or too lightly, and the message would not, therefore, perform its intended function. So the sacraments are needed to deepen the range of perception of the message. On the other side, since the sacraments are symbolic acts and should properly create deep emotion among participants, to have the sacraments replace the verbal message could permit feeling to swallow up actual content. Since the message has both content and feeling, there is, therefore, a dynamic or tension relationship between word and sacraments. Each should be alert to compensate for possible one-sidedness.

At the end of the chapter we shall consider the kind of dynamic that exists within the sacraments themselves, with special attention given to the sacrament that is variously called Communion, the Lord's Supper, the Eucharist, the Mass or the Sacrament of the Altar, and THE Sacrament. We shall argue that, in each of these ways of understanding this sacrament, there is a high-level appeal to what is noblest in man, and at the same time a frank acknowledgment of what is lowest and most sinful in man, and that the dynamic of the sacrament is to bring these two kinds of forces into open tension, and then into appropriate resolution. Far from being a repressive device, this sacrament tries to have the message get through to every dimension of psychic life.

In the sections immediately ahead, we shall examine the dynamics of the word of God metaphor. Since the very notion of God's having a saving message for man implies his love and concern (that is, the immanent dimension of God), it is essential that man not treat that message as his own possession, for from then on he would hear only the message he wanted to hear rather than the message God intends. Therefore, a tension must be maintained between the otherness of God's message (that is, the transcendent dimension of God) and the partial hearing of it of which man is capable. Breaking the tension in one direction would make us smug, and breaking it in the other direction would make us hopeless in that God would be conceived as too far away to speak at all.

Theological Intent of the Word

Some brief comments about the words for "word" and how they developed can aid us in grasping the intent of the metaphor.[1] In the development of the Indo-European languages it took quite a while to get around to words for an individual word. All the early terms referred to something said, an utterance. Only gradually and secondarily did some of them come to mean an individual word in our modern sense.

In Greek, for example, *lexis* originally meant speech in the sense of utterance or diction or style but in Aristotle came also to be used in reference either to a phrase or to a single word. In still later Greek, *lexis* became the usual way of talking about a single word. In contrast to *lexis*, the term *logos* in Greek never became a grammatical expression for a single word but was always used in the sense of a verbal expression or utterance. It is *logos* that the New Testament used in speaking about the word of God. Thus, language itself has ruled out any equation of God's word with single words or phrases.

The same general kind of distinction between the words for word exists also in other languages related to ours. In French there is a large difference between *mot* and *parole*. *Mot* derived from terms meaning to mutter or to grunt. But what one gives the judge is his *parole* and not his *mot*. In Sanskrit the term was *pada*, which originally meant a pace or a step, then changed to mean a part or a portion, and finally meant a verse or a foot, and hence a single word.

The Greek *logos*, then, used by the New Testament as designating the word of God, is always something that lies behind individual words or phrases. Whatever the word of God may be, it cannot be individual words or phrases as such, no matter how they are strung together. The word of God must, then, be understood etymologically as intending a message, an utterance, or a communication.

The ancient Jews were the first to make extensive use of the metaphor of the word of the Lord.[2] They were also the first people who took history seriously and believed that God worked through actual historical events. There is a clear dynamic connection between these two convictions: on the one side, the belief that God works through historical events, and on the other side, the belief that the word of the Lord always tries to guide and save Israel, but that it does not always say the things that the people want to hear. If it had not been for the Jews' seeing the work of God in their own history, there would have been no incentive to listen to a word of the Lord that seemed unpalatable.

In many different situations the true Hebrew prophets (who were prophets precisely because they spoke the word of the Lord) told the people to repent, to stop worshiping idols, to be decent to widows and orphans, to return to the ways desired by the Lord. When the people were in captivity, wholly or in part, the prophets also suggested in grim tones that at least some of the hardships were due to their own actions, but that God still was ready to get them back on the proper path if they truly repented. When they were in the direst straits of all, as in the Egyptian captivity or starving in the desert, God supplied them respectively with escape across the Red Sea and with manna for food.[3] That is, God acted rather than spoke when need was greatest. God's prophetic interpreters showed the kinship between the word and the action of the Lord.

It is a reasonable assumption that many of the Jews who thanked God for getting them out of Egypt or feeding them in the desert were resistive to the communications of God's word through the prophets about their sinful ways, or the interpretation of their captivity, or other hard sayings in the word of the Lord.[4] In prophetic hands, however, the conviction was not lost that God's word, no less than his mighty historical actions, was for Israel's benefit and fulfillment.

In taking history seriously as under the sovereignty of God, even though God's purposes are partially turned aside by human sin and error, the Hebrew prophets also took seriously the question of time. God was also sovereign over time. If his people were in captivity, he would release them but in his own time. One can imagine many of them saying, "If he will guarantee to release us tomorrow or the day before yesterday, then we will repent." The true prophets would have none of this. For repentance understood so lightly and pragmatically could not possibly represent a genuine hearing of the word of the Lord.

The gift of the word-of-the-Lord metaphor of the Jews to Christianity was, therefore, very great. The basic dynamic factors remained the same. God is benevolent and does speak to mankind, and he does so in love and concern. We must sometimes hear messages we do not like, but, if these truly come from God, we should heed them both because God is in control and also because they are intended for our appropriate fulfillment. We may indeed have received God's message, but we can never assume automatically that we know what it is for tomorrow. So we must be receptive to the new light that the Holy Spirit may bring.

There was obviously one point at which the Christian dynamics differed from those of Judaism, namely, the conviction that God had sent Jesus into the world as his son, to teach and preach the word of God, but also to die in a manner that would somehow save mankind. In Christian thought Jesus became the "word incarnate," that is, the word of God in human form. Rejoicing about God's action in Jesus Christ, therefore, especially when his life and action were seen as the most basic conception of the word of God, tempted the earliest Christian churches to retreat from the hard teaching about the word of the Lord that the Jews had achieved. If it had not been for the ministry of Paul in those early days, performing for the early Christian communities the same kind of function as the true Hebrew prophets had performed earlier for Israel, the small Christian movement might never have understood that the word of God is not only the good news in Jesus Christ but is also, when necessary, the corrective of bad interpretations and sinful conduct.

Since Christianity almost from the start took in Gentiles as well as Jews, it had very early to consider what the word of God meant to individual persons. Reliance could not be put on a common heritage. Therefore, the word of God had to speak to local groups, families, and individual persons in a way that would correct their practices, bring their views into line, and in general make them open to hearing the word of God whether they liked all its content or not.

So long as the word of the Lord was addressed to a specific group, sociologically speaking, it was clear that this word included at the deepest level divine love and concern for Israel, but that it also had no hesitation in clobbering the whole nation

170

for its infractions of the covenant, and even more specifically, those members of the nation who did wrong with widows and orphans and others in need. When the sociological situation changed and Christians were not a primary group in the sense of the Jews, there was also a change in what the word of the Lord meant. It still contained an element of concern for human history. But because the Christian church was not organic in the same sense as Judaism had been, it lost some of the dimensions of self-criticism in light of the word of the Lord that had been evident in Judaism. Further, the kaleidoscopic change of Christianity from a persecuted minority movement to becoming the state religion of the empire cut down its capacities for self-criticism of its overall corporate self.[5] Reception of word-of-the-Lord criticisms became more a matter of individual persons, leading to such phenomena as the rise of monasticism. Many of the bishops in power found it hard to hear the word of the Lord in the ancient Jewish critical sense.

In both the Old and New Testaments, the Bible experimented with some other metaphors for God's revelation to man. Once in each Testament there is the finger of God, basically attempting to demonstrate God's reserve power.[6] The hand of God is used more than once, generally suggesting support but sometimes change of direction.[7] The arm of the Lord appears, generally showing God's power although always with benevolent intent.[8] These additional metaphors all had utility, but they all were of secondary value because they were purely biological, while the word of God was a combination of body and psyche.

We should remember that written language in those early days was limited to a few writers, and that most messages were heard by the ears and not seen by the eyes. This fact may have contributed to the viability of the metaphor of the word of God.

In the unique word-of-God teaching of the New Testament, Jesus appeared as the "word made flesh," as the Christ or anointed of God, or as the special Son of God. This event is represented as the logos or word behind the message, giving the message or good news its substance and content.[9] From the point of view of metaphors, the New Testament vision of Jesus as the Christ and as the word of God made flesh extended the auditory dimensions of the metaphor (hearing God) into both a visual and an empathetically tactile dimension. Now one could see Jesus on the cross and also metaphorically touch his injuries. In other words, the framework of the word-of-God metaphor was enlarged to include these other capacities of perception.

Thus, the doctrine of the incarnation, God's enfleshing himself in Jesus in order to share fully in the human predicament in order to rescue mankind, was a radical reaching out of God's word beyond any possible obfuscation in abstractions so that all men, actually seeing and touching, might grasp the intent of the word of God that had been given all along but never before in such complete and comprehensive fashion. This was and is the conviction of the Christian.

Since Jesus was regarded as in some way God in human flesh, he was an event as well as talking. So there was the word, in him, both as verbal communication and as trans-verbal communication. The sacraments emerged eventually out of the latter dimension.

The fundamental intent of the metaphor of the word of God is to point to that which, when heard and heeded and pursued, saves and guides men decisively just where they most need such help. If one is certain that, in advance, he knows everything important, then he is unlikely to be attentive to the word that God speaks. Jesus pointed to the Pharisees as a case in point.[10] They listened only to the rules as formulated in the past, and not to God's word in the living present. In contrast, what happens when the word of God is truly heard? One is not guaranteed any immediate better feeling. Indeed, truly hearing may at first hurt subjectively. But if God is God and wills well for mankind, then one can work it through until he sees how the word is genuinely for his fulfillment.

During the many recent years in which Karl Barth was regarded as the world's greatest theologian, I found it difficult to get excited about the word of God since this idea was central to Barth's thought.[11] Rightly enough, Barth wanted to pre-

172

serve the otherness of God and God's transcendence, and I have always agreed with such intentions. But Barth tended also to interpret preaching and proclamation as the primary means of utterance of the word of God, and he also was very resistive to study of reception of the word of God with any means that included explicitly modern disciplines like psychology. Consequently, I began my thinking about this chapter with some bias against the word-of-God idea, except that I recognized that the metaphor is of immense importance in criticizing human pretension and false claims to knowing what is important. I am now, quite possibly, much closer to Barth than I was at the beginning. I still disagree with him on the two points mentioned. Further, I believe that not a little of his wisdom came from unacknowledged modern sources and not exclusively from the Bible as he seemed to hold. And I think that his resolution of the word-of-God question, in the form of the best preaching possible but with only passive acquiescence at best among its receivers, is well intentioned, but also a partial travesty of what the word-of-God metaphor must intend. The great point about Barth in terms of the word of God is his understanding it through Jesus Christ and his seeing its transcendent dimensions.

Thus, I am a reluctant convert to the power and meaningfulness of the metaphor of the word of God. Dynamically understood, this is the best of all possible metaphors, despite the distortions to be discussed in the next section, for conveying the meaning of God's revelation and man's attentiveness to it.

Problems of the Word Metaphor

Through the twenty centuries of Western Christianity, the principal distortion of the word metaphor has been to confuse the words of the Bible with the word of God. Fundamentalists of all kinds and in nearly all ages have committed this heresy. Some have been petty, for instance, using Paul's side remarks about female millinery in church.[12] Others have used literal biblical words as directives concerning music in the church. Still others have wrung out of literal biblical words the notion that one ought never to become angry, or that there are no occasions when a marriage should be dissolved, or that God has less concern for the nutritional than for the symbolic values of food. And in addition to these oddities, there have of course been honest differences of conviction about what constitutes the word of God.

No one was more sensible or more influential in getting off these sidetracks than Martin Luther. The word of God, he said, is not the literal words of the Bible, or anything later in terms of laws or words. The word is, instead, he asserted, whatever "drives Christ" into the heart, makes the person take it seriously, so that he responds, repents, accepts forgiveness in Christ, and then gets on with his life. Luther had no sympathy for people who sell this main concern down the river and become obsessional about literal words of scripture here and there.[13] Of course he was right.

In addition to the main distortion, however, there have been many others. Since the prophets and Jesus and Paul all spoke up, it is very easy to interpret literal speaking up as if it were the word of God. Eduard Thurneysen, of Switzerland, relying on Karl Barth, for instance, has written about pastoral care as if its essence were appropriate preaching by the pastor to individual persons after he has heard their story.[14] But he has presented no genuine individual cases to enable us to see what he actually does. In practice, he may be very understanding. He is not against the inclusion of wisdom brought forth from modern disciplines like psychiatry in the minister's understanding. But in his theory, he seems so much focused on what the minister says when the word of God is to be brought forth that he seems to confuse the word of God with what the pastor says. On this critical question, happily, Thurneysen's view seems to be increasingly rejected even by European pastors.

The word-of-God metaphor has also been used to suggest that only one-way communication is needed between God and man, so that even prayer is nothing but an exercise in psychic acquiescence. Man is to have his radio ready at the right time, hear the instruction, and then go out and do it. When he comes back to God in prayer or worship, he is to report, but never at any cost to tell God about how full of weeds the field was that he was supposed to plant. The general notion in this position is itself hypocritical: put your best foot forward to God, or else grovel. This makes of God either a tyrant or a conspirator with psychic dishonesty.

Among the pathologies and distortions of the word-of-God metaphor we should also note those who think it necessary to receive God's word every hour on the hour, such as the followers of Frank Buchman and the so-called Oxford Group Movement.[15] At least formerly, they used to get together first thing in the morning, each with notebook and pen in hand, and write down the directions for the day that God himself dictated. If they had not been quite so sure that they had captured God in their notebooks, it would not have been so bad.

The metaphor of the word of God, especially in various Protestant forms of Christianity, has subtly but wrongly given the impression that God is Talk. Thus, preaching has sometimes been represented as being *the* medium of revelation, as if everything else including the sacraments were purely derivative. I am not attempting to denigrate preaching when well done. Communication through words is still our principal human medium of understanding, and I think God is smart enough to get this simple point. But the notion that God's word is abounding only when the Christian preacher is opening his mouth on Sunday morning is both false and offensive.

In spite of all the distortions to which the metaphor of the word of God is liable, however, there is nothing to compare with it as the principal metaphor for understanding God's revelation to man and his continuing attempts to guide man although always with respect for human freedom. What is essential has already been revealed, but since life itself moves up and down, be alert for future messages. God reveals when we cannot do it for ourselves, but he does not insult us by revealing things we know for ourselves like the multiplication table. There can be no valid teaching about revelation that denigrates human freedom, or that sees God as an authoritarian schoolmaster convinced that we will never learn anything unless he jumps in and drills us on all points.

THEOLOGICAL DYNAMICS

In reflections on pastoral counseling, and no doubt also about therapy by psychiatrists and psychologists, I have wondered whether there are elements of revelation confidently hoped for by all counselors in their counseling or psychotherapy. In their right minds, no counselors would expect such boons at any particular time. Thus, any good counselor or therapist knows that he does not control the forces and the timing that bring about such results. But using methods and processes likely to lead, at some time, to such results is the stock-in-trade of both counselors and therapists. Indeed, it is their faith.

I wonder if this faith is not, in however secular a sense, an implicit belief that the word of God will speak although not necessarily in the time span we would ideally hope for. Such a view is not dissimilar to a belief in revelation in the theological sense. The counselor must have patience, even at times near the limits of his endurance. But if he has this faith and is doing everything he can based on knowledge, then he does well to endure and wait for God's word, or its secular equivalent, to break through.

There is probably no conceivable distortion of the metaphor of the word of God, as intending the revelation of God to man, that has not found its way into actual beliefs at some time in Christian history. On distortions, history is a better teacher than imagination. Although the dynamics of such distortions are varied, they all include a penchant for wanting to know for sure and to still the doubt of possible ambiguity. Thus, the dynamics lie in deep-level problems, but, in attempts to get out of the anxiety of confronting them as such, the distortions emerge from denying the depth and coming-to-surface solutions. To be sure, all this has very little to do with hearing the genuine word of God, which is directed at precisely the depths that the distortions, in their anxiety, want to get rid of. Our comment is description and explanation and not condemnation. If the movement toward honesty of psychic life is to be sustained, there must first be acknowledgment of the psychic forces at work.

The Sacraments

The underlying meaning of any sacrament is to show that God works through events and not simply through words, however important words may be. If God is interested in the entirety of human existence, as we believe, then he wants these special symbolic events to reflect the range of human psychic life, and not to be so cleaned up or prettified that they contain only the cerebral dimensions of experience. A partial test of any sacramental act is of course its ethical character. Sacramental acts that suggest or permit unethical results—for example, leading to violence or promiscuity or superiority notions—are gravely suspect. But even if the ethical conditions are met, any sacramental act is also properly to be judged by the range of the psychic apparatus to which it is relevant.

This discussion will focus on the central sacrament in Christianity, which carries five names: the Eucharist, Communion, the Lord's Supper, the Mass or the Sacrament of the Altar, and THE Sacrament.[16] My thesis will be twofold: first, that the act itself needs to be seen from the perspective stressed in each of these names, and second, that each approach represents a dynamic and tension understanding of the human psyche to which it addresses itself. That is, the sacrament as a whole aims at articulating the tension between man's lower levels and his higher levels rather than trying to deal with the lower by repressing them. It attempts to help the lower levels to be acknowledged by the higher and, without putting undue faith in the higher levels, to serve generally as supporters of the higher levels so long as they do not attempt to deal with the lower levels by mere repression.

The first name for this sacrament is the Eucharist, which in Greek means thanks and gratitude. God is gracious. He shows grace. The grace is shown through this event. But men are weak and resent their need for grace. What the sacrament tries to do as Eucharist is not to deny the human resentment about need, but to transform it. Bring your conflicted feelings with you. No automatic solution guaranteed, but you may get a step ahead either through honest recognition of your resentment or through a bit of a new vision about gratitude. The dynamics are to bring about open confrontation of feelings so long as they are within a degree that is tolerable.

This sacrament is also known as Communion. Despite the way in which we are split off from one another and from our Lord, the sacrament always reopens the fellowship door. It means reconciliation, with our Lord and with one another. To be sure, whatever grudge or insult put us out of communion is still present. But the sacrament acknowledges this fact, touches it sympathetically, and is hopeful about change rather than condemnatory. Perhaps fellowship is not just a chimera after all. The sacrament understood as communion does not condemn us for our isolation. It lures us to move beyond our grievances into genuine fellowship.

The third name is the Lord's Supper. Here the primary reference is to the rite as following the dinner that Jesus had with his disciples on the last night of his life, which was not itself without turmoil since it was followed by Judas' betrayal of Jesus. What is emphasized here is remembrance. Jesus is very human from this perspective, eating and drinking as does any human being. We are enjoined by him, in recollection, to eat his flesh and drink his blood in remembrance of him. This injunction anticipates a bit of theological history since he was not crucified until the next day. But it links the meal with his supreme sacrifice. And the eating and drinking, while in memory of him, are also at another level of psychic life representative of the human dealing with aggression and greed. It was precisely on that night that Judas betrayed him. The appeal is to both the highest and the lowest dimensions of human psychic life. Both are touched and dealt with by the sacrament.

The fourth perspective on this sacrament is as the Mass. The origin of that word is shrouded in mystery, and Protestants have not liked it but have happily introduced in recent years the "Sacrament of the Altar" as a substitute. From the point of view of the sacrament as the Mass, Jesus is seen as the perfect atoning sacrifice. No further sacrifice to God is needed for the salvation of mankind, only appreciation of and proper participation in the work of Jesus Christ. The lower-level human psychic enemy here is the temptation to appeasement. "I was not too bad, Lord; so give me a chit getting me into the kingdom." The Mass does not deny this kind of defensive maneuver but absorbs it and attempts to transform it.

The fifth way of referring to this sacrament is as THE Sacrament. There is one other sacrament in Protestant Christianity, baptism, and in Roman Catholicism six others: baptism, penance, marriage, ordination, confirmation, and extreme unction. But the fact that we have THE Sacrament in both Catholicism and Protestantism shows the centrality of this rite in most Christianity barring a few groups like the Quakers.

In this designation of the sacrament, the intent is to show overtly the function of sign or seal. What God has revealed through the word has here been nailed down, sealed, cemented, clarified, and inscribed in the believer. The lower-level meaning dealt with by this view is the anxiety or terror of being human, of being weak in the face of decision, or being always tempted especially to retreat to safety. THE Sacrament does not fail to make contact with these lower-level motives, but makes a beginning at absorbing them into the higher-level interpretation.

Thus, in all five of the Christian names for the sacrament of the Eucharist, there is both a high-level and a low-level dimension of psychic life that is touched. What the sacrament tries to accomplish is not to blot out the low, but through enabling the high to encounter it, make possible a greater predilection toward the high. But never denying the low.

In all of Christianity the other principal sacrament is baptism. By most groups this is applied to infants, but by some, only to adults or adolescents. The principal symbolism is water. The water symbolism is generally held to mean not only cleansing and purification but also dedication and new commitment. Here also the relationship between high-level and low-level dimensions of psychic life is important. Whether baptism is done, as in my church, for infants with parents and church standing guard, or in teen-age or adulthood as in Baptist and other churches, the obligation is always to relate dynamically the wanted newness of life with the tendencies to sink back into old patterns, not to repress the latter but to bring them up into honest confrontation.

In the Roman Catholic Church as sacraments, and in the Protestant churches as rites, there are also confirmation, marriage, ordination, confession, and unction or anointing. The Protestant reluctance to call these events sacraments stems from an early Protestant decision to name as sacraments only those rites believed to be enjoined by Jesus. From my own point of view, that decision was legalistic, whatever its historical merits at the time. Even to Protestants, however, the rites that are not given the title of sacraments are sacred ways of dealing with special events especially of a developmental kind. If time permitted, I would argue that there is about each of them a high-level and also a low-level dimension, and that the intent of each sacramental act is to compel encounter between the levels and thus result in an unforced though always imperfect voluntary option for the higher level.

Our Western Christian religions have also had funerals, foot-washings, exorcisms, and many other special rites. We have even been invaded by Santa Claus and the Easter Bunny. There are obvious weaknesses in the secularization of religious events, as demonstrated by S. C. and E. B. Yet no faith can ever keep itself completely free from its culture in matters of this kind. So I am not overly against red suits or egg hunts, unless they drive out entirely the events that are being interpreted.

The central point I have been making is that sacraments or rites, in our Western Christianity, must be understood in multiple perspective, both theologically and dynamically. One may still take the events and rites, or leave them. But, either way, the decision should be made only after knowing the dynamics involved.

If Christians had family-type holidays, as the Jews have, I believe there would be more appreciation for the sacraments among lapsed Christians than there is at present. Because of their special history, the Jews learned to celebrate at home. Except for early days, most Christians never had to celebrate in secret; hence they never developed home-type celebrations.

180

Christian celebrations tend to be public and in church. The catacombs tend to be forgotten. Perhaps Christians should live as if the catacombs were always just around the corner.

A Secular Word and Sacraments?

In view of the enormous needs of our world today, theologians who are responsible cannot discharge their duty solely by reinterpreting the tradition in however dynamic a manner. They may believe deeply, as I do, and as I hope these pages have indicated, in the relevance and meaningfulness of the Western theological tradition, no matter how many criticisms need to be made of it.

But we live in a heterogeneous world. A great many intelligent men of goodwill, even if they are related to churches, and many are not, are seeking a word and perhaps even a sacrament that will speak to their condition and help them to interpret their life beyond the facts of scientific advance, technological expertise, reasonable security of income, and causes to support.

Traditional formulations are unlikely to be helpful to such persons. If my thesis is correct, the reason is not that such people are stupid or basically alienated, but rather that they have not been helped to understand the dynamics of commitment. In its proper sense, commitment is not about all the details, but is about the long-term purposes that institutionalize themselves in an organization like the church. A committer who never voices criticism misses the point. For the life of the organization cannot be sustained without serious group reconsideration of responses to criticism by committed persons.

If the church has any intelligence at all, it should be able, at least on some occasions, to package its wares so that men of goodwill may be willing to take it seriously even if they are not ready to become full members. There is no reason why compromise of conviction should be involved on the part of the church. But it is high time that the formulations of the church should not, at the very least, create such misunderstandings.

Chapter 9
THEOLOGICAL DYNAMICS

Throughout this book an effort has been made to show that a dynamic understanding of any theological teaching helps to clarify both its positive intent and distortions that have clouded that intent. Whether or not this claim has been substantiated in regard to the doctrines that have been discussed is a decision the reader must make for himself.

I am certainly not the first writer who has tried to understand theology dynamically, although I know of no other general book in theology that has pursued dynamics as its principal method of clarifying the teachings. The way in which I have used dynamics is, however, different from that of Paul Tillich in his *Dynamics of Faith* and elsewhere.[1] He began from an ontological perspective, and understood "dynamics" and "form" to be the two basic elements needed to grasp reality. In such a view dynamics includes all movement, all tensions, and everything but form. This is quite legitimate when one demonstrates, as Tillich does, exactly what he is doing.

My attempt to apply dynamics to theology arose from quite another source, mainly in dynamic psychologies beginning with that of Freud but with some reference also to dynamics in sociology. In those disciplines the forces of tension and equilibrium within and between persons and groups are studied, often along with efforts to help relieve those tensions that are so great as to cause pain or anxiety or discomfort. The forces of psychic life, and of social life as well, are not all out in the open nor are they all to be understood at a single level. Consequently, the psychological or social study of dynamics requires close attention to the specifics of any situation. As my knowledge of psychological and social dynamics developed over the years, it became increasingly clear that these insights could be useful in understanding theological teachings, but with a warning that one remain as close to specifics as possible. Thus, the level of my discussion of theology is different from that of Tillich, just as the dynamics with which I deal are more specific than his.

In dealing with faith, for example, Tillich demonstrates its necessary relationship of tension with doubt and rightly argues that faith without doubt would be anemic. Serious or existential doubt, he writes, is a confirmation of the fact that faith exists.[2] If I had had a chapter in this book on faith, I should certainly have agreed with Tillich's position so far as he goes. But as I have tried to do with other doctrines, I should have attempted a more detailed analysis of the intrapersonal and interpersonal processes and tensions out of which faith may appear. The level of theological thinking done by Tillich, and by many others in fact, does for theology important things that I could never attempt. But I believe that my "lower-case" level of analysis can make some contributions that even a Tillich did not attempt.

In the rethinking and re-articulation of theology that must be done in every age, it is my conviction that each theologian may contribute more to general understanding by open acknowledgment of his perspective and its limitations than by writing as if his were "theology in general." The details of the position he holds may in fact be far less significant than the perspective, or background slant, that he brings to the investigation.

Over the past century or two some progress has been made that would support my position as suggested above. Theological faculties have teachers in various branches of theology, divided not by point of view but by areas of technical competence. A philosophical theologian, a historical theologian, and a biblical theologian, so long as they all believe the faith to be viable, are not merely specialists in their pursuit of particular data. In principle, each of them brings a perspective to the understanding of theology today that is unique. Ideally, the contribution of each should be laid on the theological table with no illusion that its angle is superior or final. Theology should increasingly become an enterprise of sifting out contributions from various perspectives based on special competencies and slants.

Science is far ahead of theology in understanding itself as a corporate enterprise welcoming the contributions of many persons with many perspectives, but reserving the corporate right to question both the truth and the relevance of what is set forth. Not that I am interested in theology's imitating science at many other points, such as the pervasive view among scientists and technologists that if we know how to do it, we should try it. But on the specific point of acknowledging the enterprise as corporate, and thus requesting contributions from many angles, I believe theology may well imitate science.

The day is past when theologians, even by silence, could justifiably profess expertness about the whole of their discipline, and about all the modes of human knowledge that contribute to it. This statement is not intended to deny the existence of great synthesizing minds either in the present or the future. But upon analysis, every one of the synthesizing minds of past and present proves to have had a special angle or perspective from which he viewed the whole.[3] As Whitehead rightly noted, perspective elimination is impossible in human beings.[4] But we can get ahead if we request the contributor to state his angle.

Even though I have taken positions on many of the teachings discussed in this book, those positions are far less important than the method of trying to understand doctrines through dynamic analysis. For the most part my position is orthodox in the sense that dynamic analysis reveals great merit in the original intuitions. I also have some interest in moving the whole theological enterprise ahead, especially by taking process philosophy seriously.[5] But in this book, my emphasis is on understanding the teachings we already have in a dynamic way.

In what follows, I shall attempt to state what I believe theology is, with special reference to dynamics, but in such fashion that it might be clarifying to churchman and nonchurchman alike.

Theology and Religion

Whatever theology may be, it is not coterminous with religion. But at the same time, there could be no theology without a religious faith to provide its start. Let us deal first with the differences between religion and theology.

First, theology is a reflective and implicative enterprise which, no matter what its starting point, eventually gets round to certain consequences that go beyond religious practice however defined. If certain convictions are held, for instance, that God made of one blood all the races of mankind, then theology will attempt to draw out the implications, in this instance, in terms of setting aside racial prejudice. It may be that, in earlier and more tribal days, this kind of interpretation was not much articulated. But if it is a proper implication from the basic position, then better late than never.

It is quite possible for religious belief and practice to be, at least relatively, inarticulate and unreflective. Do this or that, either ritualistically or ethically, and such actions may take care of religion. To Europeans and Americans, this kind of non-reflectiveness except for a handful of scholars seems in part to characterize, for instance, Islam. And yet honesty compels us to confess that some Christian groups seem equally unreflective.

There are three essentials about the relation of theology to religion. First, there is a group and not a lone individual person or family. Certain convictions are held in common, and these are associated with certain ritual practices and are followed by certain behavioral consequences. If there were no shared beliefs, theology would simply be philosophizing by individual persons.

Second, theologizing begins, as does religion, from an awareness of the "holy" in the sense of Rudolf Otto, that mysterious dimension of life that both attracts and awes in a unique sense and which is felt to be other than ourselves.[6] Whether any or all of the "holy" is called by names like "God" or by no name at all (to follow the usual practice of the ancient Jews) may not matter. The basic religious point is the recognition, and carrying out in action, of something that is not just ourselves but that is an immensely important dimension of our lives. If there is no sensing at all of this mysterious and ambiguous aspect of life, then there can be no religion and consequently no theology following from it.

Third, theology moves from a "faith" and not simply from an experience. A faith certainly need not be a dried and abstract creed. It may well be most important as it evokes, in terms of genuine feeling, a trust in that which is trustworthy. But there can be no faith without some kind of reflection that goes beyond immediate feeling, and which has had, therefore, some kind of critical intellectual treatment. When we speak of a faith that is more than uncriticized concurrence in particular beliefs and behaviors, then we indicate that some kind of critical and reconstructive principle has been built into the faith itself.

Dietrich Bonhoeffer, who was killed by the Nazis, asserted that Christian faith should move beyond religion.[7] What he meant was that religion was a kind of purely human enterprise instead of listening to God, and that this kind of approach to faith should grow up and do for itself what it could, while heeding the word of God in genuinely basic matters.

Even though Bonhoeffer's definition of religions appears extreme, it should be clear that simply equating religion, even in a better sense, with theology will not do. Joseph Doakes of St. Mary's Church may attend worship on most Sundays, support his church financially, be kind to his neighbors and his children, and he may even read the Bible now and then. But he may also believe in a God that nearly all theologians have rejected, in an immortality they regard as unbiblical, and in a conception of love among human beings that theologians regard as repressing and denying the aggressive components of the human psyche. Mr. Doakes may be doing the best thinking he can. But we cannot equate his beliefs with normative notions of theology.

Furthermore, Mr. Doakes may believe falsely that racial or economic questions can be solved simply by working hard as he did, that there would be no mental illness if people practiced their religious faith, that international problems would all be solved if everybody were Christian, and that he loves people in an unqualified sense. Whatever his individual virtues, Mr. Doakes is oversimplifying. Thus his reflections on his religion are, at the most, a bare beginning in the direction of theology. And there will have to be much correction if they are to arrive at that condition.[8]

Theology does, then, begin and proceed from a faith base. It is group-related and not merely an individual matter. It reflects critically and does not merely echo what it has heard. And it has some principle of criticism, thus calling for reconstruction in every new age. Without some kind of theology in this sense, faith or religion tends to become merely traditional or even obscurantist. It is, therefore, theology that keeps faith and religion in touch with the changing social and personal forms of life.

Theology as Expressive of Faith

Part of the function of theology is to articulate the faith, to express it so that old members may get fresh insights, the young may understand what their parents believe, and outsiders may evince respect if not necessarily personal interest. The articulation succeeds, however, only to the extent that the basic meanings are conveyed in what is always the new and somewhat different age, with fidelity and yet with needed changes in pattern and language. Thus theology is always trying to combine fidelity with communicability, and there is never a detailed chart from the manufacturer.

It is inevitable that there should be, in every fresh attempt to express faith, a tension between the way it has been stated before and the new attempts to make its statement fresher, more relevant, or more convincing. If novelty alone is the standard, or relevance, then what emerges may be a distortion of the faith. But if fidelity is associated too closely with particular patterns of thought, then there is no novelty, and irrelevance grows. Therefore the factors must be held in dynamic tension: fidelity and relevance, theological intuition and communicability, orthodoxy and novelty.

In moving to try to express faith, theology begins from the conviction that something of great importance has actually happened. This may be regarded as positive, as Paul regarded his own conversion to Christianity; or it may be felt as negative, as the early Christians thought of the crucifixion. Either way, the events simply cried out for explanation. Theology as expressive of faith is a finding of explanations that really fit even if they are paradoxical.

A similar process seems to go on in some dimensions of ordinary life. Let us imagine, for instance, a competent psychiatric team that has imaginative leadership, genuine concern and curiosity on the part of all members, and a procedure for reflecting on its work.[9] Let us suppose further that one patient, whom everyone has tried to help and who has baffled them all, has suddenly made a real stride ahead. All are convinced that the step is positive and important. But if they are to help the patient move further in the same direction, they need to know why the present step was possible. One member may suggest, "Perhaps she got tired of walking as if she were in a space suit. It's as if she realized that she was no longer walking on the moon, and that she could safely discard this defensive apparatus."

Only time will tell whether this general line of explanation is correct. What the staff member has done, however, metaphors and all, is to try to express what may have happened in producing a shift in behavior and attitude that may mean the difference between life and death to the patient. In such realms there is knowledge but not exact science, so that the metaphors belong. But the coiner of this metaphor will not go unchallenged. Another member will raise questions. Eventually the chairman or someone else may voice what appears to be the consensus at that time after the dynamics of discussion. It is not necessary that the group understand that they have been engaged in trying to "express faith." But there is a striking similarity in the process they have undergone and that which takes place in the theological attempt to express faith.

As in the illustration, there is nothing in the theological effort that guarantees that the result is faithful to the facts or that its metaphors will communicate effectively. Many things may go wrong. As the word "dogmatic" reminds us, rigidities and blindnesses may enter, for "dogma" originally meant only a teaching. Some teachings obviously became closed.[10]

In Christianity and Judaism, which have beliefs and principles but regard them as having emerged from history and events, expressing the faith may take either of two general forms: narrating and interpreting the events, or describing and clarifying the principles. Thus the dramatic as well as the expository form of expression is inherent in these two faiths. Probably the most effective communication is achieved with some combination of the two methods. Without reference to events, principles tend to lose their connection with actual situations. Yet mere storytelling without principles to relate the meaning of the old event to the new situation makes the expression nostalgic rather than salvatory.

In this section I have tried to establish the nature of the process by which theology tries to express faith, as based on events but then also considered in terms of doctrines or principles. Special theological work has always been done by individual theologians such as Jeremiah, Paul, Thomas Aquinas, or Calvin. Inevitably, each of them spoke from his own perspective. But he also spoke from within the religious community, and tried to speak as well as he could on behalf of God. This would not have been possible for any of them if they had not participated sympathetically in the events, and been cordial to the principles, that emerged from the religious community. Thus, theologizing is done by persons, but it is a group-representative enterprise.

The articulation or expression of faith is essential to the vitality of faith itself. But the expression of faith, no matter how well it is done, does not in itself necessarily prove any claims it may make about its truth. Theology must, therefore, do something besides express its faith. As we shall indicate successively, it must undertake critical inquiry and life guidance. We shall consider these functions in turn.

Theology as Critical Inquiry

In older days of the Western world, before the Latin word for knowledge, *scientia*, had been confined to the application of particular methods in particular disciplines, theology was known as the queen of the "sciences." Such a phrase has a hollow ring in our more democratic day. But those who coined the phrase were not trying to say that theologians were the most important people. They were trying to render their conviction that the subject matter with which theology deals, namely, life and death, is most important to everybody. They put a high value on their discipline because of its ultimate relevance to everyone.[11]

Along with its attempts to express the faith, Christian theology has been unprecedented almost from the beginning in its attention to theology as critical inquiry. Inquiry may of course come in various degrees. At the most primitive, inquiry may mean only finding the loopholes and plugging them up. In the development of Christian thought, inquiry has never been so narrow as that.

Because of rapid social changes in their world, the Christians from the second through the fourth centuries had to devote major portions of their time to inquiry. A decision was made to explore the relation of Christian faith to the knowledge and opinions of the general world of the time, and not to take refuge in special knowledge that could be known only to members. Nobody knows all the reasons why this decision was made nor all the dynamics behind it. But if the decision had gone otherwise, Christianity might well have become either a small backwater group or a group sociologically such as Islam later became, using theology mainly to defend itself and not also to question and improve its own interpretations.

If the reader ever has an opportunity to hear a description and dynamic explanation of some of the creeds of the early church by some such dynamic analyst as Albert C. Outler, he should jump at the chance.[12] The early creeds were points of equilibrium in a great sea of tension, and surprisingly to anyone who has not studied them in their context, the issues they discussed are still very much alive today. A reading or recital of those early creeds today may give the impression of orthodox rigidity, or even of irrelevance. My discussion is not the place to bring those creeds alive, but I assure the reader that they

190

deserve the kind of interpretation that demonstrates this fact. Despite their deep meaning, however, I hope we have learned the lesson that particular statements of belief, even when emerging as equilibria after genuinely creative tension, ought never to be enshrined in their language. The world moves rapidly, and the next conference or council, to maintain both fidelity and relevance, will have to speak to some issues not covered by its predecessor, and will have to alter here and there what its ancestors said. Creeds (even constitutions and bylaws) are very useful when they are not ossified and can be reinterpreted in terms of their basic intent in light of new situations.

What honest theologian can deny that there have been fits and starts in genuine and self-critical honesty about theological inquiry? A gross illustration of the distortion occurred in our own lifetime in the Tennessee Scopes trial, in which William Jennings Bryan represented himself as leading the forces of Christian faith, and his opposing lawyer was not a Christian who interpreted evolution differently but Clarence Darrow, the brilliant lawyer who saw no need for religious faith. Where were all the intelligent Christian lawyers when poor school-teacher Scopes was looking for help? Later instances come to mind—some good, some not so good—of theologians engaging in honest theological inquiry even when, on the face of it, the action seems to threaten the integrity or the power of the institution they represent. I am far from alleging that theologians always take the wrong side, as in the Scopes trial, and anyhow, Bryan was a poor theologian. Often, their positions have been clearly against injustice no matter what the personal cost to them.

Nevertheless, not all the brave theologians, much less the ordinary church members, who have taken radical action on economic, racial, and other social issues, have interpreted accurately the dynamics that have resulted in their decisions nor the dynamics of the faith they claim to profess. Some of them, even if their social concern is genuine, have not succeeded in dealing constructively with the authority or parental problem in their own lives, and translated it into other spheres. Others have developed beyond such parental dependency, but insist on taking a black-white view of the problems. In both cases, whatever the merits of the cause being worked for, there is distortion at the motivational level.

It has become clear today that there can be no self-respecting Western theology that is not dialogic in character and in function. If a biblical scholar knows no Oriental languages, history, archaeology, or philosophy, he has few academic or theological legs to stand on today. If a student of Martin Luther knows nothing about the general social and political and human situation of Luther's time, he is equally suspect. Dialogue does not mean capitulating to the opinions and conventions of the cognate secular discipline, but it does mean taking seriously anything known that bears upon one's own concern, and being honest in one's treatment of it.

In theology today there are disagreements about what constitutes a branch of theology. I have argued, for instance, that there is a proper branch of theology, pastoral theology, that emerges from reflection on our attempts to help people in the light of our Christian convictions.[13] Some of my colleagues, however, regard pastoral theology as merely the application of knowledge, and thus not really a proper branch of theological inquiry. Nevertheless, in spite of disagreements, it is hard today to find any theologian in any branch who believes that he can dispense altogether with an inspection of nontheological branches of learning.

I do not mean to imply that the dialogic emphasis was discovered only in our own century. In terms of method, some of our ancestors like Thomas Aquinas were ahead of us in taking seriously all the knowledge available in their respective days. But it is only in our own day that knowledge, especially through the great expansion of research, has compelled us to see more generally the necessity of the dialogic method that we have been following, sometimes a bit haltingly, all along.

The argument in this section has been that Western theology, even though with fits and starts, has been as much involved in genuine inquiry as in expressing what it thought it had. One cannot deny the black chapters like the inquisition, the religious wars, dark treatment of the Jews, and much else. But in spite of such historical facts, and in spite also of some obscurantism, I believe that Christian theology will continue to be interested in really critical inquiry.

Theology as Life Guidance

In addition to its function of articulating the faith, and inquiring into whatever is known that may affect understanding of the faith, theology has a third function of interpreting actual living and giving guidance about it. Whether this is called ethics or something else, it attempts to guide behavior about the self, in relation to other Christians, and to everything else that exists.

Life guidance may take either of two general forms. On the one hand, it may set patterns in the sense of what is the most efficient motivational system to move people, using their freedom, toward the best of which they are capable. On the other hand, life guidance may set up detailed laws and regulations, with some means of punishing violators. Both forms have been used in Western life guidance.

Under the leadership of persons like Paul Lehmann and Joseph Fletcher, many theologians today are trying to reduce the influence of the legalistic approach to life guidance, and to work far harder to enable people to make their own decisions on the basis of a sound understanding of principle and a competent analysis of the situation they confront.[14] I am fully in sympathy with such efforts.

It needs to be recognized, however, that the dynamics of persons attempting to guide their lives in this way are very different from those who rely on outside rule or law. The legalistic person may conform, or he may rebel, in relation to any particular situation. Often he has inner tension about whether to conform or to rebel. What he does not do is to admit the ambiguity that is present in all human situations, so as to compel himself to re-examine both situation and principles, and thus come to a decision, right or wrong, for which he has assumed responsibility. Thus, the legalistic approach, in working so hard for good behavior, tends to be deficient in helping people to increase their moral responsibility. The tensions in the legalistic person tend not to be used creatively.

The dynamics of the person attempting to use the other approach are different. If he has common sense, he will of course use the guidelines from history. But he cannot allow the inner dynamics to become a simple option of conformity to or rebellion against them. He must do his best to move on the basis of the principles (like freedom and love, for instance), and to analyze the actual situation he confronts with a clear intention not to distort. If his plan is going to work, so that eventually even wrong decisions suitably reflected on may increase his capacity for responsibility, then he must accept the anxiety of never being sure he is right or wrong until later. In terms of anxiety, things are never wholly rounded off for him.

Confronted with this anxiety, and his determination to confess ambiguity rather than deny it, this kind of person has many more subtle temptations than the legalist. He may misinterpret the basic principles, try to simplify the factors in the actual situation so that it becomes distorted, or he may in fact build up a secret and idiosyncratic kind of legalism to which he conforms but never criticizes. If "situation ethics" or "contextual ethics" is going to have a chance, it seems clear that these dangers and temptations must be recognized in advance. If that is not done, then people of all ages may misinterpret this approach as simply a do-it-yourself on any-old-basis injunction, and confuse moral responsibility with license, as did the Corinthians to whom Paul had to write a sharp letter of correction.

The studies by John T. McNeill, and by William Clebsch and Charles Jaekle, make it clear that the kinds of life guidance situations that were historically recorded were mainly those in which the individual person violated the standards of the group in his behavior.[15] There was of course much more life guidance activity than shown by such records. There was help to the dying and the bereaved, to the sick, to the anxious and troubled and the guilty, little about which got into print because it did not have an issue to decide. A principal reason I am using a loose term like "life guidance" as a major function

194

of theology is to show that "ethics" and "care" ought not to be separated categorically.

A theology of life guidance mainly concerned with teaching people to obey rules, rather than to become responsible, is faulty. It is also ineffective, for it invites nonconformity as soon as the protective conditions fostering conformity have changed. I am not of course denying, even in the church, the need for some law to deal with those who flagrantly violate minimal standards of responsible behavior. But the presence of such law is only a protection against the exercise of irresponsible power. It is out of place as the principal approach to life guidance.[16]

Theologies East and West

We arrive now at a delicate part of my thesis, namely, the difference between the understanding of the theological enterprise in the West as against the East, not so much in terms of content as in relation to method and dynamics. In what follows, the reader should understand that I am not necessarily claiming the religious superiority of Christianity over Buddhism, Hinduism, or Islam. As a Christian, of course I believe Christian faith to be more comprehensive and adequate. But what is involved in this section is simply a descriptive and analytical attempt at the differences in method, conception, and dynamics of theology.

The difference comes mainly through the different weights given to theological critical inquiry. How basic is it, who is to do it, and when is the general understanding to be altered as a result of its work? All the universal religions are agreed that the faith should be articulated, and that life guidance should be given. But who must think about faith, to what aspects of the world's life should faith be related, and how important is it to inquire and not simply defend—these are the methodological questions on which the West differs from the East. Even a brief discussion may demonstrate the differences in dynamics between the two approaches, although it is bound to be restricted in view of the vastness of territory.

195

THEOLOGICAL DYNAMICS

It is probable that the root of the difference between theology in East and West is cultural rather than religious. A partial proof of this contention may be found in studies of Eastern Orthodox Christianity which, in terms of theological method, tends to be more like the religions of the Orient than like Western Christianity. Let me repeat that this is not a negative comment on the beliefs of Eastern Orthodox Christians. But, as in the Orient and in other religions, they simply do not believe that the ordinary priest or religious functionary ought also to be a critical theologian.

In Western theology, who are the inquirers supposed to be? To begin with, all the clergy or ecclesiastical celebrators are supposed also to be, in some significant sense, theologians, i.e., people who reflect on the faith and its meaning for life guidance. Although experts are always admitted, the ordinary priest or pastor cannot use their existence as an excuse for failing to confront his own obligation to think it out. Thus, at least in principle, no priest or pastor can get along simply by doing. He must also inquire and reflect. Thus theologizing is not solely for the experts, but is also for everyone specially charged to carry the faith into the world.

Early Protestant Christianity went further than the insistence on inquiry by its clergy, and urged that there be study of the Bible in every home. The general point, that every professing Christian has an obligation to study and think, and not merely to profess and to act, meant that the obligation to inquiry is inherent in the practice of the faith itself. Important as specialized theologians may be, they are to guide and stimulate the theologizing of other Christians and not treat their own work as exclusive. Details aside, Jews as well as Christians in the West have some obligation to study their faith and not merely to practice it.

In their conception of theology and who is to do it, the other great religions of the world are quite different. In Islam the education of the people who conduct worship to be also thinkers and inquirers is only now beginning. In the Far East there are gurus, Zen masters, and other leaders who certainly include inquiry beyond their functions of expressing the faith and giving life guidance. But their clientele is only a small minority and essentially aristocratic, which partly explains why it appeals to some Westerners. It may not be an accident that, until very recently, the comparative scientific study of religions has been done only in the West.

An even more subtle aspect of the methodological difference between East and West in relation to theology may be seen in *Asian Psychology*, by Gardner and Lois B. Murphy, an illuminating volume summarizing the ideas about human beings that characterize the Far East.[17] Without apology, many of their data are taken from those classics that must be regarded as religious, philosophical, moral, and psychological at the same time. The Oriental languages generally do not have words for religion or for theology in our Western sense. People in the East may look on this point with pride, believing that the West has tended to separate things that belong together. Who knows the extent to which they may be right?

But the clustering together in the East of theological, philosophical, moral, and psychological matters has meant that Eastern scholars and practitioners have a hard time understanding what Western theology is about—as it tries to take a clear stance in faith, but then inquires as honestly as possible into everything else as it affects the understanding of faith. In the modern Orient psychology and the other behavioral disciplines are gaining ground, and one suspects that eventually distinctions will be made as in the West.

The appeal of Oriental thought for many Westerners has been based partly upon the apparent Eastern integration of theology, philosophy, ethics, and psychology. Integration is a dynamic lure, especially when it is so conspicuously absent from our own correlative disciplines. But even in confessing our own divisive shortcomings, we need to ask whether the Orient has not simply resisted an articulation and separation of disciplines needed to get ahead with any one of them. To be sure, it is tragic if separation means that there is not later any reintegration. But maintenance at the level of primary integration hardly seems to be the answer. Therefore, I would insist that theology, while closely related to philosophy and ethics and other disciplines, has a unique function to perform, whether in Christianity, Judaism, or Buddhism. It is to inquire into and rethink the faith in the light of all available data, and it is to do so on behalf of all believers.

In these days when the world grows smaller very rapidly, it is encouraging to see signs of genuine discussion among representatives of the world's great religions. No man with an ounce of inquiry within him can possibly take a serious look at what other faiths stand for and simply conclude that they are wrong and that his group is wholly right. Yet I do not believe that such discussions will be helped if we try to get rid of theology in the Western sense. Content aside, the merit of our enterprise lies in its insistence upon critical inquiry as well as on the expression of faith and life guidance. Truly ecumenical discussion assumes a penchant for re-examination and self-criticism, along with defense of what, after inspection, still proves viable. On this point, I believe the East must bow to the West if we are to get ahead. But then, I am a Westerner, and on this point I may not have understood God's grace or his providential guidance.

The Context of Western Theology

"Context" is a slippery word. But in all Western theologies the context or setting or indispensable mental furniture in the background has always been the relationship between God and man.[18] On the one side, we can know nothing about God in himself, apart from what he has done in relation to the world in general and to us human beings in particular. On the other hand, whatever we may learn about man himself or in relation to other creatures, which may be important knowledge, is always biased unless it is set into the context of man's being a creature made in the image of God but at the same time being given "dominion" over the earth. And modern ecology raises a few sharp questions about man's right to deal as he has done with the other creatures.

One of the clearest recognitions of this indispensable context for theology appeared in John Calvin's statement that we may begin theology with either God or man so long as we never move a step without asking about the relation of each to the other.[19] The famous discussion by Thomas Aquinas about the relation of faith to reason was another way of asserting this context. Thomas believed that faith, if we understand it aright, may go beyond reason but can never contradict it. Mystery may go beyond knowledge, but the fact of mystery should not be an excuse for sloppy inquiry.

There were important dynamic reasons for this position about context, for instance, as stated by Calvin. On the one side, if it was believed that God was ultimate sovereign of the world, then there would be great temptation to consider views of God in himself (whether up there, down under, or anywhere else) that were not based on his prior or present action in the world and among men. Thus, purely speculative views of God, apart from the Christian revelation, might take over.

On the other side, however, any attempt to consider the human situation in foreshortened terms that excluded man's being a sinful creature saved only by God's action in Jesus Christ would lead to a neglect of the very factors that provide hope for mankind. In principle, then, Calvin's position about context prevented any sharp separation of what is known about man from what is known about God, and insisted that both be reflected on at the same time.

From the side of accomplishment, this position about context saved Western theologies, except for moments of regression, from falling into obscurantism so sure of itself that it could ignore the world and the disciplines of culture. Any true or authentic knowledge about man must be taken seriously. But since this investigation of what any discipline has found out must always be done in the light of revelation, there can be no simple baptizing of any particular philosophy (including the sciences of today) as indissolubly connected with faith in terms of their point of view.

Especially in the light of some new dimensions of knowledge such as psychology, the God-man context position may be updated to say that if a group professes to study what is ultimately important to mankind without serious study of ourselves, it is dilettante. And it implies, on the other side, that what is allegedly ourselves that fails to consider the mysterious and transcendent and sometimes holy dimensions of our lives is bound to render an inadequate account of our human situation.[20]

The insistence that the proper context for theologizing is the God-man relationship, and not either alone, does not of course guarantee that a single item of alleged content is either true or significant. Perhaps the Jews crossed the Red Sea and got out of Egyptian captivity because they were politically astute and were precocious engineers rather than because God led them. Perhaps the death of Jesus on the cross meant simply that petty Roman rulers decided to get rid of a potentially dangerous agitator while they had the chance, rather than that his death was to atone for the sin of mankind.

Theology does, therefore, require some prior faith in order to make its declarations fully intelligible. One who scorns the interpretations that God led Israel across the Red Sea, and sent his Son into the world to save it, will have difficulty in accepting the further elaborations that stem from such convictions. Nevertheless, even the scorner may be able to understand that the whole of what is being asserted, and examined into, has a dynamic basis. Tensions are acknowledged and confronted and dealt with, not by the shortcuts of magic but by religious faith and practice, augmented by the critical cutting edge of an inquiring theology.

In our day it is possible to assert that the context for theology is the relationship of man and God, just as Calvin put it, but at the same time to enter a few specifics about what it means to take that context seriously. The biblical message itself must be understood in the light of scholarship that includes historical, linguistic, archaeological, and related modern means of grasping its message. The development both of religious ideas and institutions must be examined with the aid of modern historical methods, not wholly devoid of possible bias but attempting to acknowledge it when it is inevitable. The philosophical disciplines that deal with the assumptions behind all reflective thinking must be looked at not only for their possible help in sharpening tools but also in giving theological thought a constructive base. The world is a much smaller place these days, and so the serious and sympathetic study of other religions is a genuine obligation.

But the fleshing out of the meaning of the context of the God-man relationship requires also serious attention to those modern disciplines that have studied man in himself or in his relationships, such as psychology, sociology, anthropology, economics, political science, and others. The argument of this book has been that the understanding of dynamics, while by no means the sole perspective that can illuminate the meaning of theological teachings, is nevertheless of great importance. And I have had no hesitation in showing that my original grasp of psychodynamics and sociodynamics was made possible by the psychological and sociological disciplines.

Once we have grasped the basic point of view, that theological doctrines themselves always exist in a dynamic relationship, containing tensions and equilibriums and the temptation to distortion, then we can proceed to deal with these dimensions whenever theological teachings are discussed. To some shrewd theologians I must confess that my insistence on the dynamics may appear as belaboring an obvious point. But even if they should be right, I still believe that the dynamic nature of theological doctrines is worth the risk of belaboring.

REFERENCES

Chapter 1: *Freedom and Destiny*

1. "For freedom Christ has set us free; stand fast therefore, and do not submit again to a yoke of slavery." Galatians 5:1. Or, "For the law of the spirit of life in Christ Jesus has set me free from the law of sin and death." Romans 8:2. Again, "Therefore, if any one is in Christ, he is a new creation; the old has passed away, behold, the new has come." 2 Corinthians 5:17. Also, "the free gift of God is eternal life in Christ Jesus our Lord." Romans 6:23. The rejoicing of the Gospel of John is in a more philosophical vein, but real nevertheless. "So if the Son makes you free, you will be free indeed." John 8:36. Even when the words "free" or "freedom" are not used, we sense the mood of the freedom of self-fulfillment in the use of words like "joy" and "rejoice," and in the references to freedom from bondage of various kinds.
2. For example, "you have died to the law through the body of Christ." Romans 7:4.
3. As an illustration easy for the reader to follow if he is not trained in psychology, see Sigmund Freud's discussion of obsessional neurosis in his *A General Intoduction to Psychoanalysis* (New York: Washington Square Press, paperback, 1960, pp. 271 ff.). For Freud's insightful views on the similarities and differences between obsessional neurosis and some aspects of religious behavior, see his "Obsessive Acts and Religious Practices," in *Collected Papers* (London: The Hogarth Press, Vol. II, 1950, pp. 25-35).
4. For instance, "Let no one seek his own good, but the good of his neighbor." I Corinthians 10:24. In the third chapter of Romans, Paul quotes scripture, that "None is righteous, no, not one; . . . no one does good, not even one." Romans 3:10, 12. This discussion then leads to the way in which God through Jesus Christ has justified us or made us righteous. But this act of God's has made us free, and any righteousness that comes to us is from God and not our possession.
5. See especially I Corinthians 5.
6. Although each has quite different problems, all five of the cases presented at length by Freud in Volume III of the *Collected Papers* (London: The Hogarth Press, 1950), are common in this respect.
7. I made a recent firsthand investigation of the incidence of younger hospital patients at the Menninger Foundation, the Topeka State Hospital, and the Topeka Veterans Administration Hospital. I discovered that, in all these hospitals, the proportion of patients under the age of twenty-five has increased greatly over the past few years, and that a considerable proportion of these are of the "character disorder" type. My informants assured me that this trend is nationwide.
8. Charles Reich, *The Greening of America* (New York: Random House, 1970).
9. *Alcoholics Anonymous* (New York: Alcoholics Anonymous Publishing Company, 1955 and later), Chapter 7.

10. For a penetrating discussion of termination in psychoanalysis, see Karl Menninger, *Theory of Psychoanalytic Technique* (New York: Basic Books, 1958), Chapter VII.

11. In many respects the questions about freedom as self-direction, and those about will and willing, are similar. In this connection, an excellent summary of the problems and issues about willing—in theology, philosophy, and science—may be found in the volume edited by James N. Lapsley, *The Concept of Willing* (Nashville: Abingdon Press, 1967).

12. A good modern summary of the relation between ancient Hebrew thought and the development of the Christian doctrine of creation may be found in Langdon Gilkey's *Maker of Heaven and Earth: A Study of the Christian Doctrine of Creation* (Garden City, N. Y.: Doubleday & Co., 1959), in the early chapters. The remainder of the volume is valuable as a general re-examination of creation teaching and its implications.

13. Cf. Genesis 1:28-29.

14. Langdon Gilkey writes, ". . . man was an 'image,' not a shadow of God, and this meant that he existed and could be creative in a creaturely way, as God existed and was creative in a divine way." *Maker of Heaven and Earth*, p. 61. I am more dubious when Gilkey proceeds to suggest that "biblical man understood himself as a being related more fundamentally to God than to the nature that surrounded him." *Ibid.*, p. 172. The issue lies in the meaning of "interpreted more fundamentally." Since the Jews never denied their bodies, I would hold that they maintained the dialectic very well on that side, and that their reversions tended to be from the other side of the dialectic or tension.

15. The reader is reminded that there are two accounts of creation in Genesis, one in the first chapter and the other in the second.

16. As an introduction to Augustine for the nontechnical reader, I recommend the new translation of the Confessions and the Enchiridion by Albert C. Outler: *Augustinus, Confessions and Enchiridion* (Philadelphia: The Westminster Press, 1955). Here is a typical Augustine statement about freedom, "We are then truly free when God ordereth our lives, that is, formeth and createth us not as men—that he has already done—but also as good men, which he is now doing by his grace, that we may indeed be new creatures in Jesus Christ." *Enchiridion*, par. 31.

17. A useful modern translation of Augustine's *On Free Will* is by C. M. Sparrow (Charlottesville: The University of Virginia Press, 1947). Among the many more general histories of Christian thought that include competent discussions of Augustine, that which has most influenced me is by A. C. McGiffert, *A History of Christian Thought* (New York: Charles Scribner's Sons, 1933 and later, Vol. II, pp. 71-124).

18. In the *Institutes of the Christian Religion* (Philadelphia: The Westminster Press, edited by John T. McNeill and newly translated by Ford L. Battles, and part of The Library of Christian Classics, 1960), Calvin held that the fall has deprived man of free will. Book II, II. Unless a man is helped by grace, free will in any event is not enough. II, II, 6. But Calvin speaks also of "Christian freedom," something we have after acceptance of Jesus Christ, and which includes freedom from the law, from libertinism, and from social irresponsibility. III, XIX. Luther's basically similar views on freedom and free will may be found in *Luther and Erasmus: Free Will and Salvation* The Library of Christian Classics, Vol. XVII (Philadelphia: The Westminster Press, 1969). The new Luther editing and translating was done by P. S. Watson and B. Drewery. Luther's treatise is on pp. 101-334.

19. Calvin argues that events come about not through mere fortune or chance (*Institutes* I, XVI, 2), nor fate (I, XVI, 8).
20. Perhaps the most successful of the determinists today, at least in terms of winning converts, are the psychological behaviorists, of whom the acknowledged dean is B. F. Skinner. See, for instance, his *Science and Human Behavior* (New York: The Macmillan Co., 1953).
21. This kind of position is evident in all Rollo May's writings, but is perhaps most explicit in his *Psychology and the Human Dilemma* (Princeton: D. Van Nostrand Co., 1967) with its detailed discussion of freedom and responsibility, pp. 161-221).
22. Sören Kierkegaard's understanding of freedom as a kind of two-edged sword is set forth effectively in the small volume *The Concept of Dread* (Princeton: Princeton University Press, 1946, edited and translated by Walter Lowrie). But in Kierkegaard's indirect way of writing, freedom is also discussed nearly everywhere in his voluminous publications. For the reader who wants more than the small book mentioned above, but has not the time to go through everything, I recommend *A Kierkegaard Anthology*, edited by Robert Bretall (Princeton: Princeton University Press, 1951), which contains well-chosen excerpts from virtually all Kierkegaard's writings.
23. Dorothy Baruch, *One Little Boy* (New York: Julian Press, 1952).
24. We are beginning to have a new level of discussion on the question of what minimal capacities are needed to say what a human being is. Is a child born with enormous deformities that he can do nothing for himself ever a human being? Is an older unconscious person who can never retain consciousness a human being? The answers to these questions are ultimately ethical, but science contributes data to understanding them.
25. The most competent recent interpreter of freedom as self-transcendence has been Reinhold Niebuhr, especially in his *The Self and the Dramas of History* (New York: Charles Scribner's Sons, 1955).
26. Paul Tillich, *Systematic Theology* (Chicago: The University of Chicago Press, 1951), Vol. 1, pp. 182-86.

Chapter 2: *Grace and Gratitude*

1. For the background of this etymological discussion I have drawn chiefly upon Carl D. Buck, *A Dictionary of Selected Synonyms in the Principal Indo-European Languages* (Chicago: The University of Chicago Press, 1949).
2. The letters of Paul are abundant in references to grace in the sense described. For example, ". . . since all have sinned and fall short of the glory of God, they are justified by his grace as a gift, through the redemption which is in Christ Jesus." Romans 3:23-24. "For I am the least of the apostles, unfit to be called an apostle, because I persecuted the church of God. But by the grace of God I am what I am, and his grace toward me was not in vain." I Corinthians 15:9-10.
3. See notes 16 and 17 of Chapter 1.
4. Although Karl Barth did not attempt to analyze gratitude in the way in which this chapter does, he nevertheless understood that gratitude is the appropriate human response to grace. At one point he wrote, ". . . the liberation of the Christian consists in the fact that he no longer has to exist in the dialectic of the moral and the immoral, but may now exist in that of forgiveness and gratitude." This is from *Church Dogmatics* (Edinburgh: T. & T. Clark, 1936 and later), IV/3 (sec. half), & 71, 6, p. 670. However, by using forgiveness (which is an action by God) along with gratitude (which is a human response), Barth does not have to proceed

with analyzing subjectively the human response. Both his insight and his limitation are also seen when he wrote that gratitude is "unconditionally and inescapably demanded of man," even though it should be "at bottom voluntary." *Ibid.*, IV/1, Chap. 13, p. 41 and p. 103.

5. Especially Calvin cited Augustine and for all practical purposes agreed with him. Thomas also cited Augustine, but his style of questioning could not be quite content with the Augustinian paradox. I have not of course forgotten the many groups, such as the Arminians and the Wesleyans, who saw the issue differently in part. But I am not writing an extensive history, only hitting the historical high spots that seem needed for my constructive argument.

6. I must confess that I have not been able to find this statement. But it is so good that it must be used anyhow.

7. For an understanding of grace from a competent scholar with an Anglican perspective on grace, I recommend *Grace and Personality* by John W. Oman (New York: Association Press, 1961). The historical work is well done for the general reader on the topic of grace as a whole. But in spite of the word "personality" in the title, it is interesting that the volume contains no section on gratitude, nor is that word even listed in the index. From the remarks made in the text, it must be clear that I believe some of my Calvinistic ancestors were misled into believing in irresistible grace not so much because of their motives in answering, but because of their motives in framing the question.

8. I am sorry that I cannot locate this statement, but it is too good to be excluded.

9. Group for the Advancement of Psychiatry, *Methods of Forceful Indoctrination: Observations and Interviews* (1790 Broadway, New York City, 10019, 1957).

10. Even in recent excellent works on grace, that make successful attempts to redomesticate it significantly in our theological thinking, some of them done by my friends, I continue to feel surprised that they make so little of gratitude. *God's Grace and Man's Hope* by Daniel Day Williams (New York: Harper & Row, 1949) is a basic work covering a wider theological scope than its title might suggest, but clearly showing the basic meaning of grace in many dimensions of man's life. But it says very little about gratitude. Charles R. Stinnette's *Grace and the Searching of Our Hearts* (New York: Association Press, 1962), with all its merits, has a few pages on gifts but nothing explicitly about gratitude or thankfulness. A promising Catholic volume by William W. Meissner, who is trained psychologically as well as theologically, is called *Foundations for a Psychology of Grace* (Glen Rock, N. J.: Paulist Press, 1966) and takes the principal psychological correlates of grace to be identity and a new understanding of the virtues. Although I am sure the connections he makes are relevant, he has almost nothing to say about gratitude. Paul Tournier in *Guilt and Grace* (New York: Harper & Row, 1958) writes trenchantly as usual in a sermonic vein, but I cannot see that he has done anything about gratitude as response to grace at least in an analytical sense. Indeed, winsome as Tournier is, he has never done much systematic analysis of anything. It may very well be that my focused attention on gratitude and its pathologies, in considering the human response to grace, will prove to require supplementation. But I cannot see how we can even make a serious beginning at analyzing response unless we take gratitude, in its various forms, seriously. So far as I can see, however, only Barth shared something of my position on this point. But his own aversion to entering into "psychological" dimensions prevented him from following it up.

Chapter 3: *Providence and Trust*

1. For example, Theodore de Bèse (usually called Theodore Beza in English), an able man who became head of the Geneva Academy, came to hold that God had decided that man (in Adam first) was going to fall even before he actually fell, and hence man's fallen state was a part of the eternal plan of God. This is the interpretation offered by the authoritative John T. McNeill in *The History and Character of Calvinism* (New York: Oxford University Press, 1954, p. 263). Arminius and others rejected such teaching. For if God had made advance allowance for the fall, then he must in some sense have caused it or have been a passive collaborator in it. And if so, what happened to his goodness, unless you were willing to limit his power?

In *Reformed Dogmatics* (New York: Oxford University Press, 1965, part of A Library of Protestant Thought), John W. Beardslee III has brought together writings of a representative sample of three seventeenth-century Reformed or Calvinistic theologians. He selected three men: Wollebius, Voetius, and Turretin—none household words to later ages. But in relation to issues like providence and predestination, and other questions as well, Beardslee's book shows the tightening and rigidifying of Calvinistic thought in the century, more or less, after Calvin's death.

2. Albert C. Outler, *Who Trusts in God: Musings on the Meaning of Providence* (New York: Oxford University Press, 1968). With the combination of commitment and sophistication that Outler always demonstrates, the main thrust of his book is a cogently reasoned argument that we still can trust in God, while both appreciating and fending off all kinds of analyses by all kinds of modern theologians who are less sure either that there is a God or, if there is, that we can trust him. As an exercise of great analytical power and communicative ability, this is a superb small book. But using so much of his energy on the problems and the other writers, Outler has short-changed his own constructive position, which is worth far more than the few pages he devotes to it. I elect to quote him in one of his off-beat constructive remarks, "The ground for our belief that the battle is worth our best is not that God is above it calling the shots, but that he is *in* it sharing the blows—*and that he is going to win it*, for us men and our salvation" (pp. 107-8). To be sure, in this statement as in the whole book, providence is understood both in terms of God's participation in human affairs (immanently) and cosmically (what will happen to us and the world?). This in itself is a tremendous insight, that perhaps there are these two dimensions of God's providence that we must keep equally in our sights. My one regret about Outler's treatment of the topic is that he used nine-tenths of his ammunition working up to a constructive point, and then, undervaluing what he had constructively, called it "musings." In the name of the Lord, I call on him to write a constructive treatment starting where he left off with this one!

3. In addition to that of Outler, another competent modern reconsideration of providence may be found in Roger Hazelton's *God's Way with Man: Variations on the Theme of Providence* (Nashville: Abingdon Press, 1956).

4. Dietrich Bonhoeffer, a brilliant young German theologian, spent a year in the United States during the early part of the Hitler regime and then elected to return to Germany where he worked in an underground theological school. He was eventually put in a Nazi concentration camp and was killed not long before the war ended. A prolific writer before his imprisonment, he also succeeded in writing in prison and getting the work out to friends. His full stature was not realized, however, overshadowed as it was by his martyrdom, until the 1950s. Among his books are his incompleted but still

powerful *Ethics* (New York: The Macmillan Co., 1949), *The Cost of Discipleship* (New York: The Macmillan Co., 1949), and *Letters and Papers from Prison* (New York: The Macmillan Co., 1953).

5. Luke 15:11-32.
6. This is the question on which the discussion by Outler, see note 2 above, is especially helpful in view of the modern questionings of it.
7. According to Exodus 16:35, the people ate the manna for forty years. One suspects that there may be a bit of hyperbole in this statement because surely somebody must have found a fig or an animal or a fish or something else over that long period. And we can wonder about the niacin and iron content of manna as an exclusive diet.
8. This report comes from James A. Michener, in *Kent State: What Happened and Why* (New York: Random House, 1971; condensed version in *Reader's Digest* for March and April, 1971).
9. The dynamic and multi-level conception of motivation is well illustrated in *The Vital Balance* by Karl Menninger, Martin Mayman, and Paul W. Pruyser (New York: Viking Press, 1963).
10. This distinction was early illustrated when Moses was on the mountain conferring with the Lord. The Lord had a lot to say, and the people became dismayed when Moses did not return. So they asked his brother, Aaron, to collect all the gold rings available, and to make a golden calf which they might worship, since they had lost confidence in Moses and in the God who was even then giving them, through Moses, the laws on tablets of stone. The Lord told Moses what was happening, and on his return he burned the calf, generally stormed around, and interpreted to the people the punishment that God would bring upon them because of their sin. Through this process the people presumably learned something about the difference between their needs (for a God who would guide them, but in his own way and in his own time) and their wants (having a god they could manage in their own way and when they wanted to). Exodus 32.
11. Karl Barth—I have searched both my memory and Barth's writings and have been unable to find his discussion of Lot that impressed me so much when I read it.
12. Genesis 19:15-30.
13. Genesis 19:30-38.
14. Erik H. Erikson, *Childhood and Society* (New York: W. W. Norton, 1950).
15. For example, see René Spitz, "Anaclitic Depression," *Psychoanalytic Study of the Child* (New York: International Universities Press, 1952, Vol. 2); J. Bowlby, "Separation Anxiety," *International Journal of Psychoanalysis*, 41 (1960); Anna Freud and Dorothy Burlingame, *Infants Without Families* (New York: International Universities Press, 1944).
16. See note 9 of this chapter.
17. An authoritative discussion of this matter may be found in Lois B. Murphy's *The Widening World of Childhood* (New York: Basic Books, 1962). This volume reports on study of a sizable group of normal children over a period of several years, from birth until some time in adolescence. The material for Charles W. Stewart's *Adolescent Religion* (Nashville: Abingdon Press, 1967) was drawn from the data accumulated by Lois Murphy and her colleagues.
18. Dorothy Baruch, *New Ways in Discipline* (New York: McGraw-Hill, 1949).
19. I should like to give this psychiatrist the credit he deserves, but because of the way I have discussed this situation, anonymity seems indicated.

20. The best-known account is by Viktor E. Frankl, *From Death-Camp to Existentialism* (Boston: Beacon Press, 1959). My comments have drawn more, however, from conversations with other persons who were in concentration camps.
21. See Anna Freud, *The Ego and the Mechanisms of Defense* (London: The Hogarth Press, 1937), pp. 117 ff.
22. Gustav Aulén, in *The Faith of the Christian Church* (Philadelphia: The Muhlenberg Press, 1948), sees correctly the relationship between trust and providence, although the context in which he discusses the relationship is almost entirely the problem of evil.
23. A new and knowledgeable way of approaching the question of providence in relation to freedom as self-direction has come from William G. Pollard, who is both a nuclear physicist and a priest of the Episcopal Church, in his *Chance and Providence: God's Action in a World Governed by Scientific Law* (New York: Charles Scribner's Sons, 1958).
24. Calvin was clear that belief in God's providence does not relieve us of responsibility. *Institutes* I, XVII, 3.
25. Precisely because the Christian believes in the providence of God rather than in mere fate or chance, he feels joyful trust, said Calvin. *Ibid.*, I, XVII, 11.
26. But Calvin himself guarded against going too far in that direction. See *ibid.*, I, XVI, and I, XVII.
27. An interesting illustration of such a trend, in an otherwise generally competent book, may be found in *Growing Up Straight*, by Peter and Barbara Wyden & Day, 1968). The book is about homosexuality, and the authors have taken account of virtually all the significant research that has been done, small as that is. But their overtone in writing to parents is the implication that parents can prevent a homosexual pattern from emerging in a child by this and that means. The fact is that our knowledge is very far from being able to give such guarantees. Hence, in the context of the present discussion, the appeal of the book is to the unconsciously and secularly predestinarian parent somewhat inclined to cast himself in the divine role.
28. See note 1 above.
29. Paul Tillich, *The Interpretation of History* (New York: Charles Scribner's Sons, 1936).

Chapter 4: *Sin and Sickness*

1. "For I know my transgressions, and my sin is ever before me. Against thee, thee only, have I sinned, and done that which is evil in thy sight." Psalm 51:3-4. Jeremiah, speaking the word of the Lord, said, "I will cleanse them from all the guilt of their sin against me, and I will forgive all the guilt of their sin and rebellion against me." Jeremiah 33:8.
2. "Though the wicked sprout like grass and all evildoers flourish, they are doomed to destruction for ever." Psalm 92:7.
3. Ezekiel, speaking for the Lord, says, ". . . though I say to the wicked, 'You shall surely die,' yet if he turns from his sin and does what is lawful and right, if the wicked restores the pledge, gives back what he had taken by robbery, and walks in the statutes of life, committing no iniquity; he shall surely live, he shall not die. None of the sins that he has committed shall be remembered against him; he has done what is lawful and right, he shall surely live." Ezekiel 33:14-16.
4. Karl Menninger writes, in *The Vital Balance* (New York: Viking Press, 1963), p. 33, "The object of the process of diagnostication is not the

collecting and sorting of pretty pebbles (although even this may be of some scientific value in large-scale epidemiological studies). It is, rather, to provide a sound basis for formulating a *treatment* program, a planned ameliorative intervention." In my terms, I believe Menninger to be arguing that a treatment program without repeated diagnostic efforts is likely to be obscurantist, and that a separation of diagnostic efforts from the continuing efforts at treatment is professionally irresponsible.

5. See notes 16 and 17, Chapter 1, about Augustine. Unhappily the brilliant Augustine thought of the inheritance of sin in biological rather than in cultural and social terms, which is part of the reason why the later understanding of original sin distorted the original intuition, and also got us into more trouble about human sexuality.

6. Speaking for the Lord, Jeremiah said, "Only acknowledge your guilt, that you rebelled against the Lord your God. . . , and that you have not obeyed my voice. . . ." Jeremiah 3:13. If this is done, then "I will give you shepherds after my own heart. . . ." Jeremiah 3:15. "I acknowledged my sin to thee, and I did not hide my iniquity; I said, 'I will confess my transgressions to the Lord'; then thou didst forgive the guilt of my sin." Psalm 32:5.

7. See especially John T. McNeill, *A History of the Cure of Souls* (New York: Harper & Row, 1951); and *Medieval Handbooks of Penance*, by John T. McNeill and Helena M. Gamer (New York: Columbia University Press, 1938).

8. The two most recent and competent books about guilt that include theological and psychological insights, are by James A. Knight, *Conscience and Guilt* (New York: Appleton-Century-Crofts, 1969), and Edward V. Stein, *Guilt: Theory and Therapy* (Philadelphia: The Westminster Press, 1968). Among theologians who first took note of the psychiatric findings about guilt, the first was probably Lewis J. Sherrill, *Guilt and Redemption* (Richmond, Va.: John Knox Press, 1945). A later book of a similar type is John G. McKenzie, *Guilt: Its Meaning and Significance* (Nashville: Abingdon Press, 1962).

9. Charging that psychoanalysts and most other psychiatrists and psychologists try simply to relieve or eliminate guilt feelings, O. Hobart Mowrer has contended that what is needed with all of them is genuine repentance followed by restitution. In my judgment, Mowrer has misunderstood the extent to which the persons he criticizes are as much concerned about real guilt feelings as they are about those that are displaced. See his *The Crisis in Psychiatry and Religion* (Princeton: D. Van Nostrand Company, 1961), and his *The New Group Therapy* (Princeton: D. Van Nostrand Co., 1964). A minister who has been a student of Mowrer, David Belgum, although not demonstrating the one-sidedness of Mowrer's position, has nevertheless come close to it in his *Guilt: Where Psychology and Religion Meet* (Englewood Cliffs, N. J.: Prentice-Hall, 1963). The merit in the Mowrer and Belgum positions is their insistence that real guilt be dealt with on its own terms. But in maintaining such a point, there is not the slightest reason for setting aside the hardwon insights about how many guilt feelings may mean something other than surface appearance.

10. Reinhold Niebuhr, *The Nature and Destiny of Man* (New York: Charles Scribner's Sons, 1941), Vol. 1. pp. 93-122.

11. After writing the text of this statement, I went back to reread Thomas on sin in an excellent new Latin-English edition of the *Summa Theologiae* (New York: McGraw-Hill, 1969, Vol. 25). It is now nearly forty years ago since I read the whole Summa. I found that the point made in my text is still generally valid but that I had, over the years, been making

Thomas a little more modern than the facts warrant. He did write this, which is in general support of what I have written about his position in the text, "A human act is human because it is voluntary, whether it is internal, e.g., to will or to choose; or external, e.g., to speak or to act" (p. 23). Thus, willing, choosing, speaking, and acting in the ordinary sense are all actions, as my text argues. Further, Thomas considers carefully whether something that one does not do is to be construed as an act, and he concludes that "a sin of omission does involve a previous or concomitant act" (p. 21). Therefore, I conclude that the words in my text are essentially accurate, but because of their brevity they fail to do full justice to the context in which Thomas saw the problems. This possible accuracy with qualifications is reinforced by my renewed conviction of Thomas' attempt to keep sin within the realm of the voluntary, whereas in modern days we see the voluntary coming not as yes or no but in various degrees from full command to involuntary compulsion. Nevertheless, Thomas is clear that "a man can sin either by doing what he should not do, or by not doing what he should do" (*ibid*). That certainly means that *actus* as needed for sin is not merely the English "action."

12. "If you are willing and obedient, you shall eat the good of the land; but if you refuse and rebel, you shall be devoured by the sword; for the mouth of the Lord has spoken." Isaiah 1:19-20. Ezekiel, speaking for the Lord, says, "I have set her in the center of the nations, with countries round about her. And she has wickedly rebelled against my ordinances. . . ." Ezekiel 5:5-6.

13. II Samuel 13.

14. This was David's son Absalom. The story is long, beginning with II Samuel 15.

15. One of the first modern scholars to see the connection between political patterns prevailing at any particular time, and certain forms given to doctrine at that time, was Shailer Mathews. See, for instance, his *The Atonement and the Social Process* (New York: The Macmillan Co., 1930).

16. Reinhold Niebuhr, *The Nature and Destiny of Man* (New York: Charles Scribner's Sons, 1941), Vol. 1, Chapters VII, VIII, IX. Another competent though brief general modern analysis of sin is by Aulén, *The Faith of the Christian Church* pp. 259-88. Aulén is, however, more narrowly Protestant than Niebuhr in his analysis.

17. On aggression, Karl Menninger's two books are still classic: *Man Against Himself* (New York: Harcourt, Brace, and Company, 1938), and *Love Against Hate* (New York: Harcourt, Brace, and Company, 1942). Generally regarded as contributing greatly to the understanding of human aggression are the conclusions of Konrad Lorenz from his studies of animals, *On Aggression* (New York: Harcourt, Brace, and World, 1966).

18. "Avoid the godless chatter and contradictions of what is falsely called knowledge, for by professing it some have missed the mark as regards the faith." I Timothy 6:20-21. The phrase itself is seldom used in the New Testament. Instead of the capsule phrase, what we find is the very sharp differentiation between the man or group who now know they are in Jesus Christ and accept the responsibilities consequent upon this new condition, and those who waver or misinterpret it, or, in modern slang, who "fudge."

19. For detailed evidence, see note 7 above.

20. For much of the material on which these statements in the next paragraphs are based, I am chiefly indebted to Philippe Ariès, *Centuries of Childhood: A Social History of Family Life* (New York: Alfred A. Knopf, 1962, translated by Robert Baldick).

21. Perhaps the reason he conveyed the idea of sin to many people was that he

never headlined it. In some of his books, "sin" never appears in the index. A good book for getting at his estrangement understanding of sin is D. MacKenzie Brown's *Ultimate Concern: Tillich in Dialogue* (New York: Harper & Row, 1965), which is based on conversations with Tillich.

22. Kenneth R. Mitchell suggested this idea to me in a letter commenting on the manuscript's first draft.

23. Reinhold Niebuhr, *The Nature and Destiny of Man*, pp. 228-40.

24. In my recent rereading of Thomas Aquinas on sin, I was impressed again with his serious warnings against the classification of sins as more or less serious, and his insistence that all sin is sinful. Thus, more than I had recalled from my original reading of him, his position on sin is close to that taken later by the Protestant Reformers. *Summa Theologiae*, Vol. 25, pp. 59-93.

25. This general kind of position, always tempered by Thomas Aquinas, is to be found, for instance, in Thomas Slater, *A Manual of Moral Theology* New York: Benziger Brothers, 1908, 2 vols.). It is also present in a much later work by Henry Davis, *Moral and Pastoral Theology* (New York: Sheed & Ward, 1938, 4 vols.). In actual Catholic practice and teaching great changes are going on, but I was surprised to discover that Robert Dailey's *Introduction to Moral Theology* (New York: Bruce Books, 1970— now aff. with Macmillan although containing some new content) contented itself with the old categories. One of the great leaders in this field is now Bernhard Häring, especially in his recent two-volume work, *Toward a Christian Moral Theology* (Notre Dame, Ind.: University of Notre Dame Press, 1966). Häring even has one chapter on "Dynamics of the Christian Life." Clearly, there is more going on orally in changing the rigid traditional pattern of Catholic moral theology than is yet evident in the literature, except for Häring and a few others.

26. If you look up "moral theology" in the catalogue of the great Speer Library of Princeton Theological Seminary, it will direct you to examine instead the category of "Christian Ethics," with an overtone that you pursue the Catholic rather than the Protestant dimensions of Christian ethics.

27. Seward Hiltner, "The Seven Deadly Sins," *Pastoral Psychology*, 9, 81 (February 1958), pp. 41-45.

28. Anton T. Boisen, *The Exploration of the Inner World* (New York: Harper & Row, 1936 and later).

29. Galatians 5.

30. I made this classification originally in my *Preface to Pastoral Theology* (Nashville: Abingdon Press, 1958), Chapter 6.

31. Karl Menninger *et al.*, *The Vital Balance* (New York: Viking Press, 1963).

32. *Ibid.*

33. Probably because he has published so far only a few articles and not also a book, Gotthard Booth has not made the impact that is deserved for his views in these matters. One of his articles is "Disease as a Message," *Journal of Religion and Health*, vol. 1, no. 4 (July 1962). Booth's title means not only that an illness should set us to some new levels of self-examination, but also that an acknowledgment of weakness (without throwing in the sponge of course) may itself be a source of new strength. Booth's insights are very penetrating and subtle and sometimes unorthodox; so I urge him here again, as I have done in person, to lay them out in a book. Generally in line with Booth's point as illness offering a message, but lacking in Booth's caution, is Aarne Siirala's book, *The Voice of Illness* (Philadelphia: Fortress Press, 1964). Even with a foreword by Paul Tillich and an introduction by Booth, this book cannot hide its propensity to use the

author's knowledge of the relationship of illness to personality patterns, and apply it rather globally to races, nations, and cultures. As analogies, the latter may have their points. But the author rather insists that if we understand one level of his discussion we are obliged to accept the others. If only Siirala had kept this book at the level of Booth, then he could have gone off into international relationships in another book with profit to all. As it is, he weakens his thesis by lumping everything together, analogies being treated as if they were literal and inherent.

34. I published an article on this subject, "Mental Health: By the Finger of God," in *Mental Hygiene*, 56, 4 (October 1963), pp. 546-51. It was also published in *Pastoral Psychology*, 15, 144 (May 1964).

35. The Gadarene story is found in Luke 8:26-39.

36. In Jung this suggestion is to be found all through his writings, in line with his basic conviction that the forces of evil (at least some kinds of factors that appear evil) are to be confronted and assimilated, and not repressed or ignored. Data on his conviction may be found in *Psychology and Religion: West and East* (New York: Pantheon Books, 1958—now taken over by Princeton University Press). Many others of Jung's writings also make the same point. While one's life is in no way to be turned over to demons, they are to be encountered, because the result of a genuine encounter can be enrichment of the path toward one's genuine individuation.

Paul Tillich understood an important distinction between the demonic and the satanic. The latter was, whether it actually existed or not, complete and unmitigated evil. What we actually confront, however, is the ambiguity of the demonic. In the sense of Booth (see above), the demonic has a message for us. The question is whether we hear the message and move beyond the demonic albeit having truly heard it, or instead blindly fight it, or pretend we are ignorant of it. Cf. Tillich, *The Interpretation of History*, for references throughout the book.

In his popular *Love and Will*, Rollo May also deals with the demonic in the general fashion of Tillich but with some other thoughts more like those of Jung (New York: W. W. Norton, 1969).

37. Obesity was also used in an article of mine, "Christian Understanding of Sin in the Light of Medicine and Psychiatry," *Medical Arts and Sciences*, vol. 20, no. 2 (1966). This article was developed out of a lecture delivered at Loma Linda University.

38. My first major publication about the relationship of religion and health was *Religion and Health* (New York: The Macmillan Co., 1943). I have returned to this subject in recent years with several articles. One is "The Bible Speaks to the Health of Man," in *Dialogue in Medicine and Theology* (Nashville: Abingdon Press, 1967), pp. 51-74. Another is "Salvation's Message About Health," *International Review of Missions*, LVII, no. 226 (April 1968), pp. 157-74.

Chapter 5: *Church and Community*

1. Paul's main discussion of the church as the body of Christ appears in I Corinthians 12. There, the emphasis, beyond the corporate metaphor itself, is upon the conviction that there are "varieties of gifts but the same Spirit." This chapter is the principal source for the discussion in the main text. But there are many other passages in Paul's letters, although briefer, to the same effect. For instance, "For as in one body we have many members, and all the members do not have the same function, so we, though

many, are one body in Christ, and individually members one of another." Romans 12:4-5. It would be very difficult indeed to consider Paul's conception of the Christian community and rule out the metaphor of the body of Christ.

2. The great modern book on this subject of homeostasis is Walter B. Cannon's *The Wisdom of the Body* (New York: W. W. Norton, 1932).

3. The great modern leader on this question of what constitutes headship or leadership within the organism was G. E. Coghill, in *Anatomy and the Problem of Behavior* (New York: The Macmillan Co., 1929). A further brilliant development addressed to the same question came from biologist Paul Weiss in *Principles of Development: A Text in Experimental Embryology* (New York: Henry Holt and Co., 1939). Since then there have been enormous new discoveries, but none, so far as I know, negating the basic findings and conclusions of Coghill and Weiss.

4. Calvin's discussion of the church is very extensive, constituting the whole fourth section of the *Institutes of the Christian Religion*. In the modern edition previously cited, his church commentary ranges from pp. 1009 to 1524.

5. As an illustration of the immense significance or those feedback processes as essential to organic life, I note an outstanding recent book by Ludwig von Bertalanffy, *General Systems Theory* (New York: George Braziller, 1968).

6. My conviction about the importance of our analyzing "promising" in the light of modern dynamic knowledge has been accentuated by my reading of a brilliant and penetrating but still unpublished manuscript on promising by Herbert Schlesinger, psychoanalyst and psychologist, now of the University of Colorado. I am not going to give Schlesinger away by prequoting him, even though he has been kind enough to give me copies of his preliminary manuscripts. The fact is, as Schlesinger analyzes with brilliance, that promises are always risks, since they mean limitations of the future in the light of convictions in the present. Hence, any promise is a qualification upon openness to the future. For those who regard freedom as containing no limitations, it is obvious that promises in the sense of Schlesinger are impossible. Can human beings be human and not make promises in this sense? Or what happens when people make apparent promises with no ability to back them up?

7. Especially illuminating on this point, but also on the other metaphors as well, is *The Household of God*, by J. E. Lesslie Newbigin (New York: Friendship Press, 1960). Newbigin suggests rightly that the household-of-God metaphor has been used especially by the new groups or the so-called "holiness" groups.

8. "So then you are no longer strangers and sojourners, but you are fellow citizens with the saints and members of the household of God, built upon the foundation of the apostles and prophets, Christ Jesus himself being the chief cornerstone." Ephesians 2:19-20.

9. Anton T. Boisen, *Religion in Crisis and Custom* (New York: Harper & Row, 1955).

10. Romans 8:23, and Galatians 4:5.

11. As suggested in note 8 above, and in many other references, "saints" in the New Testament was virtually a synonym for members of the Christian community. A similar usage was later found in newly rising and enthusiastic churches when members called one another "brother" and "sister."

12. The school metaphor does not appear in the New Testament but came later. But through the many healings done by Jesus, and his injunction to

his disciples to heal as well as to preach, and the notion of Jesus as the great Shepherd, the metaphor eventually arose in various forms which I have christened the "hospital-school."

13. Jesus said, "The kingdom of heaven is like leaven which a woman took and hid in three measures of meal, till it was all leavened." Matthew 13:33. And Paul wrote, "Cleanse out the old leaven that you may be fresh dough, as you really are unleavened." I Corinthians 5:7. The explicit application of the leaven notion to the church came later, as it did with the idea of fire. But the Old Testament idea of the people being led at night by the "pillar of fire" perhaps gave the idea its start. Exodus 13:22.

14. The main ways in which the church, throughout its history, actually did answer this question is discussed with extraordinary clarity in H. Richard Niebuhr's *Christ and Culture* (New York: Harper & Row, 1951).

15. For instance, Jesus told his disciples, ". . . preach as you go, saying, 'The kingdom of heaven is at hand.'" Matthew 10:7. But in the same version of the Gospel Jesus said, "I tell you I shall not drink again of this fruit of the vine until that day when I drink it new with you in my Father's kingdom." Matthew 26:29.

16. Amos Wilder, *Otherworldliness and the New Testament* (New York: Harper & Row, 1954), regards it as quite false to see the people of the New Testament as interested only in another world. The New Testament can certainly not be understood if there is no eschatological framework at all, and scholars differ on the extent to which this perspective dominated. But whatever the proportions, none seems to deny that something about God's kingdom is here and something else about it is beyond.

17. In my *Ferment in the Ministry* (Nashville: Abingdon Press, 1969), I have described further the organization of the church in the second century, and defended it against the romantic thinkers who wish it might have remained as loose as it was in the first century.

18. For the general reader, an especially able account of these developments may be found in Jaroslav Pelikan's *The Riddle of Roman Catholicism* (Nashville: Abingdon Press, 1959). For the reader with a special concern for how the church dealt with people, such as those who fell away during persecution, a competent analysis is found in *Pastoral Care in Historical Perspective*, by William Clebsch and Charles Jaekle (Englewood Cliffs, N. J.: Prentice Hall, 1964).

19. See note 14 above.

20. Paul Tillich, *Love, Power, and Justice* (New York: Oxford University Press, 1954). Many of Tillich's other papers especially along these same lines were published as *The Protestant Era* (Chicago: The University of Chicago Press, 1948, translated and edited by James Luther Adams).

21. Karl Barth said that the church as community "saves and maintains its own life as it interposes and gives itself for all other human creatures." *Church Dogmatics*, IV/3, § 72, 2, p. 762.

Chapter 6: *Sexuality and Love*

1. Genesis 1:31.
2. Genesis 2:18-25.
3. See Roland H. Bainton, *What Christianity Says About Sex, Love and Marriage* (New York: Association Press, 1957).
4. Judges, Chapters 14 and following.

5. Genesis 29.
6. Genesis 38:8-10.
7. See, for instance, the story of Lot and his daughters, in Genesis 19:32-38.
8. For an excellent discussion of the biblical references to homosexuality, see D. S. Bailey, *Homosexuality and the Western Christian Tradition* (London: Longmans, Green & Co., 1955).
9. *Ibid.*, Chapter 1.
10. For example, Matthew 19:8-9. I realize that such passages may be read legalistically. But to do so seems inconsistent with Jesus' character.
11. Matthew 19:10-12.
12. I Corinthians 7:8.
13. Ephesians 5:21-33.
14. I Corinthians 7.
15. Throughout the foregoing discussion in the text, I have been helped by Otto A. Piper's *The Christian Interpretation of Sex* (New York: Charles Scribner's Sons, 1941. There is a later revised edition).
16. See, for instance, the *Satiricon* of Petronius (New York: Rarity Press, 1932).
17. I Corinthians 5.
18. H. C. Lea, A *History of Sacerdotal Celibacy* New York: 1907, 2 vols., 3rd ed.).
19. Unpublished paper by Peter Hartocollis.
20. See the remarkable book by Philippe Ariès, *Centuries of Childhood: A Social History of Family Life* (New York: Alfred A. Knopf, 1962, translated by Robert Baldick).
21. Lewis Mumford, *The Myth of the Machine: The Pentagon of Power* (New York: Harcourt Brace Jovanovich, 1970).
22. See note 20.
23. See Vernon L. Parrington, *Main Currents in American Thought* (New York: Harcourt, Brace, 1930).
24. Otto A. Piper, *The Christian Interpretation of Sex.*
25. This report is available from the Office of the General Assembly, Witherspoon Building, Philadelphia, Pa.. 19107.
26. *Ibid.*, p. 46.
27. *Ibid.*, pp. 46-47.
28. *Ibid.*, p. 47.
29. I was a member of the committee that prepared this United Presbyterian report, and I am, therefore, generally in accord with the positions taken. Theologically, however, the report grounds its understanding of sexuality in covenant theory rather than, as I have done, in creation doctrine. I admit there are dangers, as the report notes, in moving from creation. But I think they can be guarded against. I am not in disagreement with what the report says about covenant grounding for sexuality, but it is too brief to be clear.
30. Seward Hiltner, "Family Planning: A Protestant View," *Southern Medical Journal*, December 1967.
31. Seward Hiltner, *Sex Ethics and the Kinsey Reports* (New York: Association Press, 1953), pp. 40 ff., and Seward Hiltner, *Sex and the Christian Life* (New York: Association Press, 1957), pp. 72 ff.
32. Daniel Day Williams, *The Spirit and the Forms of Love* (New York: Harper & Row, 1968).
33. Anders Nygren, *Agape and Eros* (Philadelphia: The Westminster Press, 1953, translated by Philip S. Watson).
34. A new kind of look at sacrifice has been begun by some modern researchers into suicide. See, for example, Paul H. Blachly, "Can Organ Transplanta-

tion Provide an Altruistic-Expiatory Alternative to Suicide"? *Life-Threatening Behavior*, I, 1 (Spring, 1971), pp. 5-9.
35. See Bainton, *What Christianity Says About Sex, Love and Marriage*.

Chapter 7: *Death and Courage*

1. Oscar Cullman, *Immortality of the Soul or Resurrection of the Dead* (New York: The Macmillan Co., 1964).
2. Jürgen Moltmann, *Theology of Hope* (New York: Harper & Row, 1967, translated by James W. Leitch).
3. Karl Barth saw this matter correctly. To say that man "has spirit means that he is grounded, constituted, and maintained by God as the soul of his body." *Church Dogmatics*, III/2, p. 344. Calvin was closer to the Greek mode of thinking. He called man's soul "an immortal yet created essence." *Institutes* I, 15, 2.
4. I Corinthians 15:44.
5. Paul Tillich, *The Courage to Be* (New Haven: Yale University Press, 1952, especially pp. 169-70).
6. For instance, II Samuel 2:32.
7. Jeremiah 29:28.
8. At least some of the different views on this matter appeared in Paul's trial, Acts 23.
9. Paul's most extended discussion appears in I Corinthians 15.
10. I. Corinthians 15:13-14.
11. *Ibid.*, verses 43-44.
12. I Thessalonians 5:23.
13. Jaroslav Pelikan, *The Shape of Death* (Nashville: Abingdon Press, 1961).
14. *Ibid.*, Chapter 2.
15. *Ibid.*, Chapter 3.
16. *Ibid.*, Chapter 4.
17. *Ibid.*, Chapter 1.
18. *Ibid.*, Chapter 5.
19. I had my education on these matters from William Warren Sweet. See his *The Story of Religions in America* (New York: Harper & Row, 1930).
20. Evelyn Waugh, *The Loved One* (New York: Dell Publishing Co., 1948).
21. Herman Feifel, ed., *The Meaning of Death* (New York: McGraw-Hill, 1959). Elizabeth Kübler-Ross, *On Death and Dying* (New York: The Macmillan Co., 1969).
22. Fortunately, there is some creative rethinking about death being done by systematic and pastoral theologians. For example, Milton McC. Gatch does a good job of tracing historical attitudes, and makes a beginning at a modern view, in his *Death: Meaning and Mortality in Christian Thought and Contemporary Culture* (New York: Seabury Press, 1969). An excellent symposium was put together by Liston O. Mills, *Perspectives on Death* (Nashville: Abingdon Press, 1969).

Chapter 8: *Word and Sacraments*

1. Here I am indebted to Buck, *A Dictionary of Selected Synonyms*.
2. The references are legion. For instance, "And at the end of seven days, the word of the Lord came to me," wrote Ezekiel, 3:16. The true prophets like him were prophets precisely because they spoke the genuine word of the Lord, as needed by the people at any particular time.

3. Exodus 14:21 ff., and Exodus 16.
4. They even complained about the monotony of the manna diet in Numbers 11.
5. For example, see Jaroslav Pelikan, *The Riddle of Roman Catholicism* (Nashville: Abingdon Press, 1959, Chapters II and III).
6. Exodus 8:19; and Luke 11:20.
7. For example, Isaiah 10:10.
8. For example, Psalm 89:13, "Thou hast a mighty arm; strong is thy hand, high thy right hand."
9. This is a central theme in the Gospel of John.
10. Luke 11:37-44, for instance.
11. Barth, *Church Dogmatics*, I/1, I/2.
12. Paul is at his worst in I Timothy 2:8-15.
13. See Theodore G. Tappert, ed., *Letters of Spiritual Counsel* (Philadelphia: The Westminster Press, 1955). These are Luther's letters written to individual persons.
14. Eduard Thurneysen, *A Theology of Pastoral Care* (Richmond, Va.: John Knox Press, 1962, translated by Jack A. Worthington, Thomas Wieser, and others).
15. Walter H. Clark, *Oxford Group: Its History and Significance* (New York: Bookman Associates, 1951).
16. In a preliminary form, my reflections on this subject were given in "The Polysemia of the Lord's Supper," *Pastoral Psychology*, 17, 170 (January 1967), pp. 3-6.

Chapter 9: *Theological Dynamics*

1. Paul Tillich, *Dynamics of Faith* (New York: Harper & Row, 1957).
2. *Ibid.*
3. As modern illustrations, Paul Tillich came at theology with his base in ontology; Reinhold Niebuhr, with bases in history and political science; Karl Barth, with his principal base in the Bible; and several recent theologians such as Gibson Winter and Harvey Cox have come out of sociology. In older days, learning was less differentiated by fields. But we can wonder what Calvin's theology might have been if he had not had his early deep immersion in the classical Greek and Roman humanistic scholarship. I have often wondered to what extent the psychological perspective available in a particular time has been influential upon particular theologians, and have generally concluded that it is most marked in Augustine, Schleiermacher, and Jonathan Edwards. Were it not for his great versatility over many fields of knowledge, I would also include Thomas Aquinas. Perhaps these dynamic predecessors of mine would be reluctant to acknowledge my claimed kinship with them. In terms of actual performance, I am thousands of miles from any or all of them. But I think that, in terms of a perspective for getting at theology dynamically, even they would have to confess some kinship.
4. For example, Alfred North Whitehead, *Science and the Modern World* (New York: The Macmillan Co., 1928), especially pp. 102-3.
5. My great teacher on process philosophy was Bernard M. Loomer. We still have a jointly rewritten and unpublished manuscript entitled *Some Implications of Process Philosophy for Psychotherapeutic Theory*. So far, schedule has never permitted me to go back to Whitehead, along with Hartshorne (my former colleague), Wieman (my former teacher), Ogden (my former student), and John Cobb, to try to get my process principles in order and

apply them to areas of theological concern that those men have not touched. It is a great consolation to me that one of my ablest students, Paul Mickey, in his recent doctoral dissertation at Princeton, was able to do just that in his consideration of individuality from a process perspective. I hope that he will be able to prepare the essence of his work for publication.

6. Rudolf Otto, *The Idea of the Holy* (New York: Oxford University Press, 1958, translated by John W. Harvey).

7. For example, see Dietrich Bonhoeffer, *Ethics* (New York: The Macmillan Co., 1955, ed. Eberhard Bethge). The basic point is found many times in nearly all Bonhoeffer's writings.

8. The ubiquity of the Joseph Doakeses with their virtues and limitations does not deter me from agreeing with the advocates of church renewal that it is precisely such people who can do significant things, provided real change comes to them first. But I am not a romanticist, and I do not believe that laymen like Doakes can automatically and without serious theological study carry forward the real work of theology and the church unless those of us who have had the time to do the study can bring a few corrective influences to bear on the position of the Doakeses.

9. For this kind of insight I am especially indebted to my experience as consultant to mental hospitals, principally to the Menninger Foundation, but also to other institutions like the Fort Logan Mental Health Center in Denver, Colorado.

10. I have always admired Karl Barth's courage in calling his principal work *Church Dogmatics*, even though wondering whether he ignored, or simply rejected, the decline of "dogma" from its meaning of "teaching" to the popular conception of rigidity. In the short term, he did not lose by his title decision. In the long term, I believe he will lose.

11. A reconsideration of the notion of theology as queen of the sciences was done by H. Richard Niebuhr, "Theology—Not Queen but Servant." *The Journal of Religion*, XXXV, 1 (January 1955), pp. 1-5.

12. Outler's new translation of two works of Augustine has been cited earlier. But so far, he has not got into print the kind of thing he does so marvellously on the platform, in reinterpreting the issues confronted by the early church fathers.

13. Especially in my *Preface to Pastoral Theology* (Nashville: Abingdon Press, 1958).

14. See Joseph Fletcher, *Situation Ethics* (Philadelphia: The Westminster Press, 1966), and *Moral Responsibility* (Philadelphia: The Westminster Press, 1967). See also Paul L. Lehmann, *Ethics in a Christian Context* (New York: Harper & Row, 1963).

15. John T. McNeill, *A History of the Cure of Souls* (New York: Harper & Row, 1951), and William A. Clebsch and Charles R. Jaekle, *Pastoral Care in Historical Perspective* (Englewood Cliffs, N. J.: Prentice-Hall, 1964).

16. An excellent warning on this point is offered in Paul Ramsey's *Deeds and Rules in Christian Ethics* (New York: Charles Scribner's Sons, 1967).

17. Gardner Murphy and Lois B. Murphy, *Asian Psychology* (New York: Basic Books, 1968).

18. At the very beginning of his discussion, Calvin said that "without knowledge of self there is no knowledge of God," and that "without knowledge of God there is no knowledge of self," *Institutes* I, I, 1, and I, I, 2.

19. *Ibid.*

20. See Peter Berger's *A Rumor of Angels* (Garden City, N. Y.: Doubleday & Co., 1969) as a particularly pointed comment along this line.

INDEX

Abortion, 119

Accidie: and silent majority, 96-97

Adam and Eve, 25

Adams, James Luther, 15, 16, 108

Adultery: biblical view of, 128

Agape, 141-47

Alcoholism, 21, 22

Alcoholics Anonymous, 22, 47

Alienation: as metaphor of sin, 89-91; and privacy, 90

Anabaptists, 117

Anger: as sin, 94

Anselm, 27

Apple, Elaine, 16

Aquinas, Thomas, 27, 86, 94, 189, 192, 199, 209-10, 211, 217

Ariès, Philippe, 135, 210, 215

Arm of the Lord, 171

Athos, Mount, 132-33

Augustine, 203, 209; on freedom, 26-27; on grace, 40, 42-43; on pride, 87

Aulén, Gustav, 208

Authority, attitudes toward, 21

Bailey, D. S., 128, 215

Bainton, Roland S., 214

Baldick, Robert, 210

Baptism, 179-80

Baptists, 118

Barth, Karl, 62, 63, 172, 173, 174, 204, 214, 216, 217, 218

Baruch, Dorothy, 33, 204, 207

Battles, Ford L., 203

Beardslee, John W., III, 206

Belgum, David, 209

Berger, Peter, 218

Bertalanffy, Ludwig von, 213

Bethge, Eberhard, 218

Beza, Theodore, 206

Blachly, Paul H., 215

Body of Christ, as metaphor of church, 109-12

Boisen, Anton T., 96, 117, 211, 213

Bondage: concern of theology for, 24; time perspective in, 20-21; types of, 24

Bonhoeffer, Dietrich, 56, 186, 206, 218

Booth, Gotthard, 211-12

Bowlby, J., 207

Braceland, Francis J., 16

Brainwashing, 51

Bretall, Robert, 204

Brown, D. McKenzie, 211

Bryan, William Jennings, 191

Buchman, Frank, 175

Buck, Carl D., 204

Buddhism, 195

Burlingame, Dorothy, 207

Calvin, John, 27, 55, 189, 198, 218

Calvinism, 28, 55, 71-78

Cannon, Walter B., 213

Children, in medieval period, 135

Christian ethics, and moral theology, 93-94

Church, 108-24; as body of Christ, 109-12; as communion of saints, 118; as covenant community, 112-16; as fire, 119; as hospital-school, 118-19; as household of God, 116-18; as leaven, 119; mission of, to world, 123-24; as new kind of community, 120-21; offices in, 120; rise of new groups in, 117-18; and social issues, 122-24; as yeast, 119

Clark, Walter H., 217

Clebsch, William, 194, 218

Clement, 158

Clerical celibacy, reasons for, in West, 131-34

Cobb, John, 217

Coghill, G. E., 213

Communion, sacrament of, 178

Communion of saints, 118

Community: early Christian experience of, 170; early church